WE WRITE
WHAT WE LIKE

EDITED BY CHRIS VAN WYK

Stephen Bantu Biko, 1946–1977
Courtesy of *The Herald*, Johnnic Communications.

Celebrating Steve Biko

WE WRITE
WHAT WE LIKE

It is better to die for an idea that will live, than to live for an idea that will die.
Steve Biko

EDITED BY CHRIS VAN WYK

WITS UNIVERSITY PRESS

Wits University Press
1 Jan Smuts Avenue
Johannesburg
South Africa
http://witspress.wits.ac.za

This publication was commissioned by the Biko Memorial Convention and
financially supported by the Department of Arts and Culture

First published 2007

ISBN 978-1-86814-464-8

Cover, layout and design by Hothouse South Africa
Printed and bound by Paarl Print, Paarl, South Africa

History from time to time brings to the fore the kind of leaders who seize the moment, who cohere the wishes and aspirations of the oppressed. Such was Steve Biko, a fitting product of his time; a proud representative of the re-awakening of a people.

Nelson Mandela

Contents

Introduction

In paying tribute to Steve Biko I cast my mind back to two specific moments in my life.

It is a hot summer day in September 1971. I am 14 years old and in standard 7 (grade 9). I am sitting at the diningroom table in our tiny matchbox of a house in Riverlea, south of Johannesburg. The heat is almost worse than the homework I am struggling with. The front door is open for some relief. Our wire gate swings open and I hear footsteps approaching. This is exactly what I need – some distraction. It's probably one of my friends coming to chat. I don't know yet who it is but I will know any second now as the footsteps make their way up the small stoep.

It's a policeman, blond and blue and white like the South African flag, and barely out of his teens.

'Hullo, can I help you?' I say.

He ignores my greeting. 'Where's Van Wyk?' he barks in Afrikaans. He must mean my father! What has my dad done wrong?

'He's in the bathroom,' I tell the young cop.

He wastes not a moment more but turns on his heel and goose-steps to the bathroom – where he bangs on the door barking out our surname.

Suddenly there is consternation in our home. Curious, big-eyed siblings peep out from rooms and Ma comes to see what's the matter.

'Get out of there!' the cop demands.

Within seconds my father flies out of the bathroom, clothes sticking to a wet body, steam rising from him, rubbing a towel through his hair.

'*Fok!*' says the cop, stepping back from my father, '*jy's nie die Van*

Wyk wat ek soek nie!' (You're not the Van Wyk I want). He flounces out of the door, leaving behind, in place of an apology, his rudeness and the smell of his sweat.

Fast forward ten years to a hot Friday morning in January 1981. I am married and my wife Kathy has this very morning given birth to our first son. I am still in Riverlea, sitting with my two best friends in my mother-in-law's tiny yard celebrating with a bottle of wine.

The grass is green, the garden is in bloom, a peach tree is so laden with its ripe fruit that some of its branches lean into the neighbour's yard. It's a perfect day – until a car pulls up on the pavement.

A fat white policeman heaves himself out of the car and makes his way to the neighbour's door. But he's very interested in the doings of the three coloured men on the other side of the fence. And as he passes us he gives us a look of disdain and utters the inevitable remark:

'The bushmen are at it again huh – drinking your lives away.'

All three of us rush to the fence and shout out our anger. The cop is so shocked that he hobbles out of the yard. He gets back into his car, mutters a threat and races away.

Why was my reaction to a white policeman that day so different from my dad's ten years ago, I asked myself. And the answer came easily. I grew up with Steve Biko; my father did not.

When my dad was a young man the Pan Africanist Congress (PAC) and African National Congress (ANC) were banned and apartheid was a cocky juvenile growing into a selfish, greedy bully.

In the sixties and seventies our coloured township had settled very nicely into just the kind of community the apartheid government wanted it to be – poor but obedient.

I learnt quickly which entrance to the post office I should use. If an adult spoke about his or her boss, my imagination conjured up a picture of a white man. The books I read were about white people, whether they were teenage detectives or a bare-chested adventurer in an African jungle. The announcers and DJs and songs and adverts on the radio all involved white people. And if for some reason a black character appeared in a soapie, he was played by a white actor with a ridiculous Zulu accent.

The world I lived in was white, and I was not a part of it.

When I was growing up, my mother had an expression for those times when my brothers and I tried to get involved in adult conversation: 'Children should be seen and not heard,' she would say.

With their laws the apartheid government went one step further, saying, 'Non-whites should neither be seen nor heard.'

Like the black American writer Ralph Ellison observed, I was an 'Invisible Man'.

When I *was* mentioned it was by the prime minister as a problem, as in 'the coloured and African problem'.

Once or twice, in a barbershop, somebody would dare utter the name 'Mandela' – but this would be followed by a chorus of loud shouts of 'Shut up! Wanna get us into trouble?'

There were, of course, men and women who were different. But they were regarded as oddities, freaks.

A man living in the next street was banned. I didn't know why nor would anyone tell me. 'He must've done something terrible,' I concluded in the absence of a reasonable explanation.

A history teacher began talking politics, but was fired or relocated or something, I don't know what. All I know is that one day he was there saying, 'apartheid is wrong'. And the next day he was gone.

A student had gone home to tell his parents, the parents complained to the principal, the principal alerted the department (of Coloured Affairs) and the history teacher was history.

There is an old African proverb that says: 'It takes a village to raise a child.' But apartheid would call for more than a mere village. It needed a village plus Steve Biko.

And Steve Biko came to me in the seventies. The first words of Black Consciousness I ever heard or saw was this simple phrase, printed in a newspaper as a caption below a photo of one Hlaku Rachidi, a BC activist: 'We are not carbon copies of white people; we are human beings in our own right.'

I stared at the text. This was a new thought, but at the same time so old that I felt I had known it for centuries longer than my 18 or so years. At about this time I became acquainted with the poetry of the Chilean poet Pablo Neruda. In his poem, 'Poetry', he describes his feelings at the moment when poetry first entered his soul, feelings similar to mine upon discovering Black Consciousness:

> I wheeled with the stars
> My heart broke loose on the wind

I was black. I am black. I am a person too. I am not invisible. I am here. But I was not unique. More and more black South Africans were becoming militant and proud to be black as the philosophy swept off the university campuses where it had begun, like Neruda's wind. In fact, here is a wonderful linguistic coincidence: in IsiXhosa, Biko's mother tongue, the word for wind, *moya*, is also the word for spirit. And so it was that this new spirit was abroad – on the campuses, in the high schools, in the township streets.

It was palpable, visible and dynamic – dashikis, afros, clenched fist salutes, students on the march, a renaissance of militant theatre, poetry and the arts.

In 1977, when Biko died, I wrote this poem:

> He fell from the ninth floor
> He hanged himself
> He slipped on a piece of soap while washing
> He hanged himself
> He slipped on a piece of soap while washing
> He fell from the ninth floor
> He hanged himself while washing
> He slipped from the ninth floor

He hung from the ninth floor
He slipped on the ninth floor while washing
He fell from a piece of soap while washing
He hung from the ninth floor
He washed from the ninth floor while slipping
He hung from a piece of soap while slipping

I read the poem in township and church halls in Riverlea, Soweto, Lenasia, Braamfontein, Cape Town. The audiences were appreciative and angry. But lurking amongst them were the apartheid government's security police. They picked me up one day and took me to John Vorster Square in Johannesburg. They had brought me here to interrogate me. But first there was a little game they needed to play out. They took me up to a ninth floor office and to a window overlooking the city.

'So, when did you see anyone falling from here?' they asked me. And 'why did you write that poem?'

I wonder if they would have understood the answer, which is that I had written the poem because Biko had died – but more importantly I had written it because he had lived. Biko's Black Consciousness had given me the courage to speak out.

As a storyteller I am moved as much by the stories of our struggle for liberation as by the philosophies that drove it. One of those stories is about the great PAC leader Robert Mangaliso Sobukwe, a man whose courage and intellect inspired Biko himself.

In 1963 Sobukwe was imprisoned on Robben Island. But so afraid was the government of his power as a leader that it separated him from the other prisoners.

Sobukwe lived alone, surrounded by prison guards day and night, forbidden to interact and talk with fellow prisoners. Every day other PAC prisoners would pass by his enclosure on their way to and from the quarry. Under their mute gaze Sobukwe would pick up a handful of sand and slowly let it trickle through his fingers. In this way he was reminding them that, 'this land is our land'.

And then there is the image of Biko that his son Nkosinathi recalls in his introduction to a recent edition of *I Write What I Like*.

> My mother tells me that he [my father] would stay up late reading and writing stuff ... [H]e would be facing the ceiling and think aloud while she took notes. Mostly, she says, there was no need to ... edit these – he had a way with words.

2007 is the 30th anniversary of Biko's death. To mark the occasion the Minister of Science and Technology, Dr Mosibudi Mangena, commissioned me to compile an anthology of essays as a tribute to the great South African son. (Minister Mangena is also President of the Azanian People's Organisation [Azapo], which is the torchbearer of Biko's philosophy.)

The contributors are President Thabo Mbeki, Minister Mangena himself, writer and journalist Darryl Accone, journalist Lizeka Mda, cleric Bokwe Mafuna, newspaper editor Mathatha Tsedu, academics Jonathan Jansen, Mandla Seleoane, Achille Mbembe and Saths Cooper, Azapo Member of Parliament Pandelani Nefolovhodwe, Azapo National Chairman Zithulele Cindi, labour facilitator Duncan Innes and Director in the Ministry of Science and Technology Veli Mbele.

The essays cover a wide range of key moments during a significant period in South African history, both personal and public: being on trial with Biko, talking with him about his philosophy and his vision, listening to him speak from a podium.

Some of the contributors never met Biko face to face but their accounts are nevertheless interesting as they describe the moment when Biko's philosophy captured their imagination as it swept through a generation hungry and eager for a new and dynamic way to fight oppression.

We Write What We Like proudly echoes the title of Biko's seminal *I Write What I Like*. In his most often quoted essay – one we have included in this book – Biko writes:

> We have set out on a quest for true humanity, and somewhere on the distant horizon we can see the glittering prize. Let us march forth with courage and determination, drawing strength from our common plight and our brotherhood. In time we shall be in a position to bestow upon South Africa the greatest gift possible – a more human face.

Today we can show the world a more human face. It may not be a face we are all proud of yet – thanks to rampant crime, corruption, and our lacklustre commitment to fighting HIV/Aids. But at least now we have the power to mould the face into one we can be proud of.

Our freedom has given me the space to write about the ordinary people in the communities in which I was raised: the housewives, the washerwomen, shebeen owners, petty thieves, schoolteachers, shopkeepers and factory workers. And in writing about them I have shown them that they are not onlookers and passersby who watch as others make history, but that they, too, make history. In my memoir, *Shirley, Goodness and Mercy*, I celebrate the ordinary people, the villagers who raised me.

We Write What We Like is a tribute to that man who came along and helped the village raise me. It is also a gift to a new generation which enjoys freedom from one who was there when that freedom was being fought for. And it celebrates the man whose legacy is the freedom to think and say and write what we like.

Chris van Wyk
October 2007

Acknowledgements

In preparing this book for publication, we were fortunate to have the excellent services of David Lea as proofreader and HotHouse South Africa as cover and book designers. We offer our special thanks to Pat Tucker for copy editing the manuscript and to the Steve Biko Foundation for allowing us to reproduce the essay, 'Black consciousness and the quest for a true humanity' originally published in *I Write What I Like* by Steve Biko (edited by Aelred Stubbs, published by Heinemann, London, 1979). Emilia Potenza of the Apartheid Museum was extremely helpful in the process of photographic research.

The publishers and I wish to thank all those institutions whose publications and archives have been cited and photos reproduced. Acknowledgement has been cited accordingly at each instance.

Steve Biko – a timeline

1946

December 18: Stephen Bantu Biko is born in Tylden, in the Eastern Cape, to Mzimgayi and Alice Nokuzola Biko.

1951

Biko's father dies.

1965

Completes his high school education at Mariannhill, a Roman Catholic mission school in KwaZulu-Natal.

1966

Enrols as a medical student at the University of Natal, Non-European section in Wentworth, Durban.

Joins the National Union of South African Students (NUSAS), a non-racial student body dominated by whites.

1968

Grows frustrated with NUSAS's reluctance to adopt a more radical stance.

Together with black students breaks away from NUSAS. Forms the black South African Students' Organisation (SASO) at Turfloop in Limpopo and is elected President. SASO's primary mission is to address the inferiority complex of black students.

Biko begins to write prolifically in the SASO newsletter under the pseudonym Frank Talk.

1970

Marries Nontsikelelo (Ntsiki) Mashalaba.

1972

Focuses increasingly on activism and neglects his studies. Is finally expelled from the university.

Begins to work with the Black Community Programmes (BCP) in Durban. The BCP addresses the problems of black workers, whose unions are not recognised by the government.

Biko and his fellow activists see the need for a Black Consciousness organisation that will operate beyond university campuses.

The Black People's Convention (BPC) is launched.

1973

The government bans Biko for five years, prohibiting him from speaking in public, writing for publication or travelling. He is restricted to King William's Town in the Eastern Cape

Despite being banned, he helps create various grassroots projects including the Zanempilo Clinic.

1975

Forms the Zimele Trust Fund (for the support of ex-political prisoners) and the Ginsberg Educational Trust. Is detained for 137 days and released without being charged.

1976

The South African Students' Movement, influenced by the BCM, is formed at high schools throughout the country.

June 16: Students launch protests against the imposition of Afrikaans as a medium of instruction in black schools. The result is the 'Soweto uprisings', which spread throughout the country.
Biko is elected Honorary President of the BPC

He is a key defence witness in the Saso/BPC trial, which runs from 31 January 1975 to 21 December 1976. The nine trialists are sentenced to long jail terms on Robben Island.

1977

Biko is arrested in March, detained and released.

Arrested again in July and released after a few weeks

August 18: He is arrested at a police roadblock outside King William's Town. He suffers a severe head injuries while in police custody and is chained to a steel window grille for a full day.

September 11: Police load Biko, naked, onto the back of a Land Rover and drive him 1 200 km to prison in Pretoria.

September 12: Biko dies in prison. Justice Minister Jimmy Kruger tells Parliament, Biko's death 'leaves me cold'.

September 25: Funeral in Ginsberg township, attended by thousands, despite police attempts to stop and harass mourners at roadblocks.

October 19: The government clamps down on the Black Consciousness Movement, banning black newspapers, *The World* and *Weekend World*, and detaining hundreds of BC activists and other government opponents.

1978

After an inquest into Biko's death the attorney-general of the Eastern Cape states that he will not prosecute any police involved in Biko's arrest and detention.

1994

27 April: South Africa holds its first democratic elections.

1997

At the Truth and Reconciliation Commission five former security policemen admit to having been involved in Biko's death and apply for amnesty.

2003

7 October: South African Justice Ministry officials announce that the five policemen accused of killing Biko will not be prosecuted because there is insufficient evidence.

Dr B Zondi (left) presents academic awards to Steve Biko (centre) age 17 and Sizo Mazibuko at St Francis College Mariannhill, KwaZulu-Natal in 1966.

Courtesy of St Francis College, Mariannhill.

Young medical students in 1966. From left to right: B Savage, R Ragavan, Ben Ngubane and Steve Biko. Soon after enrolling, Biko focused increasingly on his political activism at the expense of his studies. As a result he was expelled. Dr Ben Ngubane is currently serving as South African Ambassador to Japan.

Courtesy of the National Archives and Records Service of South Africa.

I.

Lizeka Mda

Dear Steve

Dear Steve,

It is amazing that it has been 30 years. Seems like yesterday that my eldest sister beckoned me from the playground to tell me: 'Steve Biko is dead'; that the next day, 13 September, the *Daily Dispatch* carried a full colour portrait of you, and alongside it the words: '*Sikhahlela indoda yamadoda*' ('We salute a hero of the nation'); that it was not too long ago that an ox cart carried your coffin to the funeral.

Was it only 30 years ago that the farce that was the inquest into your death opened in Pretoria on 14 November; that the general public caught the first glimpse of such unsavoury characters as Colonel P J Goosen of the Port Elizabeth Security Police and the men who disgraced their profession by covering up for the police – Doctors Ivor Lang and Benjamin Tucker, district surgeon and chief district surgeon respectively for Port Elizabeth?

It was a time, however, when the likes of Sidney Kentridge, George Bizos and Ernest Wentzel served the legal profession with honour, representing your family.

It took a Supreme Court ruling to force the South African Medical and

Dental Council to hold an inquiry into the conduct of the two doctors, in which they were found guilty of professional misconduct, in 1985. Much of the credit for that goes to Dr Wendy Orr, a very young doctor who was a subordinate of Lang's.

Your death caused ripples in our world. The world outcry was such that the apartheid government was under siege and reacted the best way it knew, by banning a number of individuals, organisations (including SASO and the BPC) and newspapers on 19 October.

With all this name dropping you would be forgiven for presuming that I knew you or that you should know me. Not so.

I was a little girl when you died and was even littler when you were making your mark on this country's political landscape. But I have made up for that by reading a lot about you.

To think that you were not yet 31 when you died. Yet you could come up with some of the insights you did, about black people, about the oppressive apartheid regime, about human nature, about the liberation movements and about the merits and demerits of capitalist and communist philosophies. Not to mention your understanding of Black Consciousness (BC).

I ask myself how you could have been so smart when you were 19, 22 or 30 and I do not have an answer. You are one of a trio I consider geniuses. You, like the other two, died so young, yet gifted humanity with a legacy for all time.

The other two? Martin Luther King Jr, who died in 1968 aged 39, and Bob Marley, 36 when he died in 1981. Geniuses. Which does not mean I don't have questions about your reputations as 'ladies' men'.

What? That's none of my business? You are my elders?

If you had lived, yes. But of course you know that you will be forever young, gifted and handsome.

If you lived during these times you might be surprised to find that people in their thirties call themselves 'youth'. You would roll about laughing if you knew that, neh? We laugh too, otherwise we would have to cry, as it is not funny at all, just an excuse not to be responsible.

That way, these so-called youths can continue to make endless demands on society, dragging everyone along on a guilt trip so that should the 'youth' fall off the rails it will be society's fault.

They obviously have no concept of what John F Kennedy meant when he said: 'Ask not what your country can do for you, ask what you can do for your country!' I want to believe you would be telling us the same now. Because, as Dr Mamphela Ramphele can tell you, instead of young people following your collective example when you set up clinics, such as Zanempilo, we have to import doctors from countries like Cuba. That's because our own people are not prepared to serve rural communities.

What about the youth formations of established political organisations, I hear you ask. Surely these are the intellectual incubators of these organisations, or at worst, disciplined revolutionaries?

That's what you think, Steve? The only way to use 'intellectual' in relation to this lot would be in the phrase 'intellectually bankrupt'. 'Disciplined'? Perish the thought!

You once said, 'You are either alive and proud or you are dead, and when you are dead, you can't care anyway.'

I hope you were right. For your sake anyway.

Otherwise you might be a little upset if you could see some of your ex-comrades. Ex? Yes! Many of them have sold out their principles and are permanent fixtures at the trough of greed and corruption that has engulfed our land. They remind me of 'Hlohlesakhe', the one who was only interested in stuffing his own stomach. Were you still alive when that drama was aired on Radio Xhosa? The belief then was that Hlohlesakhe was a parody of K D Matanzima.

Your decision back in 1969 to break away from the National Union of South African Students and form SASO resonated for many of us when we were university students in the 1980s.

But that was another place and another time. Then, one's notice board had your picture sitting happily alongside those of Nelson Mandela and Robert Sobukwe. It was a tolerant time when everyone's contribution was acknowledged, and appreciated.

We live in a different time now. There is heavy reluctance to credit people like you and Sobukwe for your role in the struggle against oppression, colonialism, apartheid.

Sometimes I think it's a good thing you died before you might have

3

disillusioned us. Because I have to tell you, a fog of disillusionment coats many of the people we idolised then. In time they have proved to be men of clay – *amadod' omdongwe*.

More often, however, I wish you were still alive. These are times when it seems that, had you lived, the philosophy of Black Consciousness would have taken deeper root; times when black people project such violent forms of self-hate one despairs for this country. Not only do we harm and kill each other as adults, we also live with the regular rape of infants. Evidently, we haven't outgrown the things 'the system' taught us. Unlike you.

Of course you saw this dehumanisation of black people when you said: 'Blacks under the Smuts government were oppressed but they were still men ... But the type of black man we have today has lost his manhood. Reduced to an obliging shell, he looks in awe at the white power structure and accepts what he regards as the "inevitable position". Deep inside his anger mounts at the accumulating insult, but he vents it in the wrong direction – on his fellow man in the township, on the property of black people...

'All in all the black man has become a shell, a shadow of man, completely defeated, drowning in his own misery, a slave, an ox bearing the yoke of oppression with sheepish timidity.'

Do you remember that self-help thing the Black Community Programmes ran? The self-reliance they taught? We've completely lost what that is about.

Now people build houses, neglect to put up water tanks and then cry: 'The government must bring us water!' Even when the government has built them houses, *for free*, the money that could have bought a water tank goes on things like giant television sets that fill up the tiny space.

Grown men see nothing wrong in appearing on television and crying: 'Our local school has no toilets; we are waiting for the government to come and build toilets!' I ask you...

And when the government does build those toilets, do you know that the cistern tanks and taps disappear in no time, into the homes of the very children who go to the schools? Did I mention before that black people can get on your nerves?

There is one person I have to credit for making you better known to me – Donald Woods.

As you well know, in the Eastern Cape of the 1970s, the *Daily Dispatch* was often the only source of information about what the Nats didn't want known. And it was all thanks to the integrity of the man who edited the paper – Donald Woods.

He could very easily have chosen an easy life and pretended that all was perfect in this land. That's what many editors did, and what many of us, faced with the might of the apartheid state, would have done too.

However, Woods was so moved by your discussions about what the BC movement sought to achieve – remember that first meeting when you summoned him to your office in King William's Town? – that he gave up the easy road for the difficult path of pointing out that something was rotten in the land of B J Vorster.

And for his dedication in speaking out against your killing – in the process forcing Jimmy Kruger to drop the ludicrous 'death by hunger strike' story – he was banned, placed under house arrest and his family was harassed and eventually hounded out of their home and country.

Donald Woods' *Daily Dispatch* one of the main reasons why I am a journalist today. My father bought it every day and it would eventually be recycled in our pit latrine in place of loo paper. So there were plenty of opportunities to read it.

Do you know that there were people who went out of their way to criticise Woods – claiming that he was using your name to build his own profile?

His *Daily Dispatch* introduced us to journalists such as Thenjiwe Mthintso, Vatiswa Ntshanga, Lulama Jijana, Charles Nqakula and Mono Badela. It was the *Dispatch* that introduced ordinary folk to another of your comrades, Mapetla Mohapi, who wrote a BC column for the paper. There was shock when Mohapi died in a Kei Road police cell on 5 August 1976 – according to his jailers, he 'hanged himself'.

There was unease, but one also got the impression that there was a belief that 'they' wouldn't go so far with a person with as high a profile as you. Surely they couldn't believe they could get away with that?

How wrong everyone was. The Nats proved that there wasn't anything they couldn't do in defence of white privilege. They took just a year to dispatch you too. Part of the outrage over your murder was the carelessness with which a precious jewel like you had been handled; the thought of what had been done to you to cause the head injury and brain damage ... to induce a coma; the idea that when the state doctors examined you, you were 'naked, lying on a mat and manacled to a metal grille'; that with those injuries, you were dumped in the back of a police van, naked, for a 1 200 km journey to Pretoria.

And they brushed off the world's disgust as if flicking off a fly.

'Biko's death leaves me cold,' said Justice Minister Jimmy Kruger, while Prime Minister B J Vorster dared the world to 'do its damndest'.

Black people, as you well know, can be a trial. They are often quick to criticise those who get off their backsides to do something, while they themselves are sitting in the sun.

That's why they could throw stones at Woods for publicising your life and work, and exposing to the world what life was like for South Africans.

I had the joy of meeting and being befriended by Woods in the 1990s. I found him to be gracious and generous. He also had a playful streak, as when he would phone me and disguise his voice, speaking accentless isiXhosa. What a silly man! I liked him a lot and was sad when he died in 2001.

I had an opportunity to see your killers during amnesty hearings of the Truth and Reconciliation Commission (TRC) in Port Elizabeth in September 1997.

What is the TRC?

It's too long a story, Steve. If you could, I would suggest you Google it. Suffice to say, it is one of the best things to have happened in this post-apartheid South Africa.

In his application to the Amnesty Committee, retired security police Major Harold Snyman blamed Colonel Piet Goosen, his commanding officer in 1977, for the instructions to keep you naked and to deprive you of sleep and food. Snyman said it was the same Goosen who had instructed the investigation team to lie about the circumstances leading to your death in statements to Major General Kleinhaus, who investigated your injuries, and to the inquest into your death.

As I reported in the *Mail & Guardian* of 12 September 1997:

> Throughout Snyman's testimony, his co-applicants Gideon Nieuwoudt, Daantjie Siebert, Johan Beneke and Rubin Marx, who were members of the interrogation team Snyman led, did not give any indication that they agreed or disagreed with their former colleague's recall of events...
>
> Nieuwoudt, on the other hand, alternated between staring into space while supporting his chin with his left fist, and looking around the hall as if trying to recognise people – his victims perhaps? He drank a lot of water and kept pouring water for Snyman.
>
> 'Why is he so thirsty? Did he pour even one glass for Biko?' the question came from an angry member of the audience.
>
> Magistrate Marthinus Prins, presiding at the inquest, ruled that Biko's head injuries emanated from the reported scuffle and his death could not be blamed on criminal offence by anyone. All lies, insisted Snyman this week as he presented what he said were the true facts...

George Bizos SC, back in your corner after 20 years, did not allow Snyman to get away with much, particularly blaming everything on the dead: you, Colonel Goosen and General Hendrik van der Bergh.

> 'The policemen did nothing wrong?' he asked. 'They acted in self-defence to protect themselves from an attack from Mr Biko? That is what your story is?'
>
> Snyman: That is correct. We had to restrain him.
>
> Bizos: If your story is true, you and your colleagues did nothing wrong. Mr Biko caused his own death and you and your colleagues are blameless?

Eventually, after much futile prodding, Bizos put it to the 69-year-old pensioner that he wouldn't answer the question because he could not answer it honestly. The tedium of the long-winded cross-examination was relieved by the vigilant audience which provided some well-timed jeers, making sure the amnesty applicants were not in any doubt about opposition to their application, even though that will not count in the decision of the amnesty committee of the commission.

But perhaps the most enduring image of that first day of hearing is of the pitiful figure of Snyman, dizzy from the relentless questioning by Bizos, pleading with his lawyer, and eventually the amnesty committee that 'Ek is moeg' [I am tired], that he is an old man who is suffering from a number of ailments, that he cannot go on. What a reversal of fortune for the all-powerful police officer of the 1970s and the 1980s, to find himself begging for mercy from three black men making up the committee. He was shown mercy and the hearing was adjourned.

The Amnesty Committee eventually rejected the men's applications. In a statement, the committee concluded:

In any event, we are not satisfied that the Applicants have made a full disclosure as further required by the Act (Section 18 of the Promotion of National Unity and Reconciliation Act No. 34 of 1995). Applicants' version as to the cause of the scuffle and the manner in which Biko sustained the fatal head injury is so improbable and contradictory that it has to be rejected as false.

Moreover, none of the Applicants has impressed us as a credible witness. They have clearly conspired to conceal the truth of what led to the tragic death of Biko soon after the incident and have persisted in this attitude before us. This has been exposed in the thorough cross-examination by Mr Bizos.

Suffice it to say that in view of the above exposition of their versions, we are not satisfied that the Applicants testified truthfully to the events leading to the injury of Biko. It appears more probable that Biko was attacked after Applicants did not take kindly to his arrogant, recalcitrant and non co-operative attitude particularly exemplified by his occupying a chair without their permission to do so.

This attack appears to be actuated by ill-will or spite towards Biko. This view is reinforced by the cruel and inhumane manner in which Biko was treated after he sustained the fatal injury, in particular the manner in which he was shackled to the metal grille and his transportation to Pretoria.

You would have been 60 this year. But in our hearts, you will always be 'Forever Young', to borrow from the lyrics of Bob Dylan, 'always doing for others', 'courageous', standing 'upright and strong'. And of course, 'your song will always be sung'.

Peace,
Lizeka Mda

Biko with fellow activist Mamphela Ramphele outside the East London Magistrate's Court where he had appeared for breaking his banning order. This photo was taken in the mid-seventies.

Courtesy of the Manuscripts & Archives Dept. of the University of Cape Town Libraries.

2. Mosibudi Mangena

Thirty years on and not much has changed

It was just after supper on a hot summer night in 1970 and the dining hall, which doubled as a venue for general student meetings and cultural activities at the University of Zululand (fondly known as Ngoye), was filled to capacity. I was twenty-three years old and studying for a Bachelor of Science degree.

Two students from the University of Natal Black Section walked in and took their seats on the makeshift podium. One was slim and bespectacled, the other tall and imposing. They were introduced as Charles Sibisi and Steve Biko, the President and Vice-President of the newly formed South African Students' Organisation (SASO). This was the first time I saw Steve Biko in action. Later, after the formal meeting, some of us retired to the student common room to engage in informal conversations with the visiting pair and I had a chance to engage with him personally.

For weeks before this meeting students at the university had been debating vigorously the merits of a blacks-only student organisation, as represented by SASO. Even among those who had accepted the motivation for such an organisation there were some who felt that Indians were sufficiently privileged by the race stratification of the apartheid system to justify exclusion from membership of the organisation.

However, the overwhelming view was that all the oppressed must stand together in solidarity and that they should not allow the practice of different kinds of discrimination to sidetrack them. None of the different components of the black community (Africans, Indians and coloureds) had a say in the degree of their own oppression. It was the white regime alone that parcelled out whatever privileges it desired to the different racial groups. Therefore, black people, as defined to include Africans, coloureds and Indians, must provide the force to bring the evil system down.

Steve and Charles called on the student body to affiliate en masse to the organisation through their Student Representative Council and, after a vigorous debate, the mass meeting voted to affiliate centrally to SASO.

With this decision, Ngoye became a strong and vibrant centre of student political activism in the country. Together with the Universities of the North, Durban Westville, Western Cape, Fort Hare and Natal Black Section we set out to re-engage the black community in the struggle for its own liberation. The banning of the African National Congress, the Pan Africanist Congress and the South African Communist Party in 1960, the imprisonment of hundreds of political leaders and activists on Robben Island, and the exile of many others, had left the oppressed population paralysed with fear about anything political. Nine years later, student activism under the banner of SASO ushered in one of the most exciting and exuberant political periods in the country.

The goal, as expressed in the SASO founding documents, was to create a free and open society where the colour, race and origin of an individual would not be a point of reference. But to get there, black people would need to reclaim their dignity and assert their humanity, which had been eroded by many centuries of living under an oppressive and racist system. Black people had to rid themselves of the inferiority complex induced in them by the pervasive lie peddled by their oppressors to the effect that they are inferior beings with ugly features, an undesirable skin colour, a backward culture and unworthy languages.

We embarked on a massive conscientisation campaign to liberate blacks from psychological oppression as one of the important pre-conditions for physical liberation. The offensive was first directed at the students themselves through debates, seminars, workshops, leadership schools, poetry, drama, essays and books.

We affirmed and elevated our African names in order deliberately to negate the trend whereby these names were sidelined in schools, churches, and the workplace. As part of this campaign we urged black women to stop lightening their skins with chemicals and straightening their hair in an attempt to cast themselves in the image of someone else. 'You are beautiful as you are,' we said.

We called ourselves Blacks and demanded that society and the media stop referring to us as non-whites or non-Europeans – we are who we are, we declared proudly, not a negation of another race or people. Although newspapers and advertising agencies at first resisted, they later understood our reasoning and relented. That was a major psychological victory for us. It was not long before we began calling our brothers and sisters by their African names. Abram, Godfrey and Aaron were replaced with Onkgopotse, Mathatha and Mosibudi.

SASO mobilised the black community to confront the white racist power structure in all its forms. The sheer magnitude of the task led to the formation of other black organisations such as the South African Student Movement for high school students, the National Youth Organisation for youth out of school, the Black Workers Project for the working class, various others for community development workers, and the Black People's Convention, an overt political organisation. Of course, the government banned all these organisations on 19 October 1977, just a month after Biko's murder in detention.

Biko, one of the most gifted, committed, sincere, sociable, intelligent and humble people I have ever known, was at the centre of all these activities. After leaving Ngoye I had become active in the Pretoria branch of SASO and later travelled around the country as National Organiser of the Black People's Convention so we met informally many times – at conferences, workshops, seminars and parties – Biko loved to party.

I would watch him listening patiently to anyone who came to him with a problem, frequently suggesting a solution that, once he pointed it out, appeared so obvious one was embarrassed not to have thought of it oneself.

His humanity was so extraordinary I could not understand why anybody would want to kill him, but perhaps it was precisely those attributes we found so attractive that were threatening to the regime.

The Black Consciousness Movement conscientised literally millions of people, particularly the young, who discovered their humanity and dignity, and lost their fear of the white establishment. It was the militancy of these cadres that led to the events of 16 June 1976. Many of them later went into exile to swell the ranks of the older liberation movements. At home, large numbers were arrested, more than doubling the political prison population. Today, three decades on, many are to be found in important positions in the political, educational, religious and business life of our country.

Ironically, while physical liberation has been attained, black people have regressed terribly with regard to psychological freedom. We worship others at our own cost and exhibit classical inferiority complexes in our day-to-day existence.

Switch on your television set at any time and hop through the channels and you are likely to see others rather than the majority of the people in this country or the continent of Africa. Move your radio dial around and the chances are your ears will be filled with music from elsewhere rather than from your own culture. To add insult to injury, we put one week a year aside to appreciate our own music. Only a people with an extremely low opinion of themselves would do something so grossly insulting to themselves.

Every aspect of our culture and values is being questioned – not by others, but by ourselves. *Lobola, koma* and *ukwaluka* (Sesotho and Nguni terms for the rite of passage), traditional leadership and our languages, which are the carriers of these attributes, are all under intense scrutiny. No other group is subjected to this much pressure and doubt about itself in this era of democracy.

Just one example is the SABC's decision to broadcast the controversial drama, *Phantsi Komthunzi Wentaba*, which contemptuously vandalises African cultural practices. They would not dare do that to any other racial or religious group in this country. But more telling, no other group in South Africa would do that to itself.

Apparently the values and cultural practices of everybody but us are fine. Perhaps that explains why we are content to see other people on our televisions and to listen to their music more than to our own. Travels all over the world teach that while many nations tune into the music and culture of others, they appreciate their own more.

The African component of the black population is the only group in this country that is eager, and perhaps even feels privileged, to have its children taught by others. It is not because we lack teaching skills, but that we won't do it for ourselves. Our own experiences at the hands of black teachers and the few islands of excellence in our contemporary schooling system prove that they can teach as well – or as badly – as anyone else.

The majority of black schools are poorer today, in terms of both physical health and educational ethos, than they were under oppressive rule. This is because communities do not take care of the schools in their midst and the professional authorities responsible for those schools couldn't care less. It is as if the adults in these communities are in a conspiracy against their own children. Basically, we lack pride in and fail to identity with what is ours.

The truth is that the vast majority of us are still suffering from a colonial mentality. Blacks in positions of authority are often ignored, undermined, and even threatened if they insist on doing the right thing. That is why our schools, hospitals and other similar public institutions have deteriorated in the past few years despite receiving more funding than they did under apartheid. Those of us suffering from this disease are not inclined to respect authority exercised by another black person and we certainly do not feel we should render excellent service to other black people.

Subliminal self-hatred induces us not to serve those who look like us with love, dedication and pride. The afflicted have no qualms about going home at the end of the day and collecting a salary at the end of the month without applying themselves sufficiently and honestly to their jobs. How do black teachers feel when parents remove children from neighbourhood schools and send them to far away schools to be taught by others because those parents have no confidence in them?

How do black teachers feel when they spirit their own biological children away from the schools at which they teach? They have no shame in admitting to their own kids that although they are professionally trained to teach, they are nevertheless not good enough to teach their own children.

And of course these children whom we fail to teach and train properly end up being under-prepared for both tertiary education and the world of work. The result is a vicious cycle of under-capacity and inability to contribute fully to the development of our own country.

If one considers that what is said about teachers applies, with minor modifications, to the majority of other black professionals the picture is very grave indeed. Political freedom might be won, but it seems that yesterday and today are one, if today is not worse, in as far as psychological liberation and group self-esteem are concerned.

Why is it that in a country where 90 per cent of the population is black, almost all the racial abuse and discrimination we hear of is perpetrated by a small white minority against this vast majority? How come blacks are the only ones being beaten up or even killed for racist reasons? Why is it not the other way around?

These things should not be happening. But if they are, they should mirror the demographics of our society. They don't, because the many centuries of oppression and systematic indoctrination have left many black people in awe of whites. You do not discriminate against or attack those you worship. It appears criminals are more liberated than most in this country because they attack and rob everyone, regardless of colour or race. It is a perverse notion, but one that stares us in the face.

It might be argued with a great deal of credibility that, because whites still have almost total control over the economy and the land, it follows that they are the only ones with the power to discriminate against blacks. You turn someone away from a hotel or bank or restaurant or give them shoddy service purely on the basis of their colour only if you have the power to do so.

The political arrangement in the country is no longer inimical to black economic participation and advancement but the problem is that black people do not support one another in economic and commercial activities. If we black people were to buy from one another, patronise the services provided by our professionals and help build the economies of our communities our fortunes would be changing for the better much faster than is the case presently.

If 90 per cent of the population were in economic solidarity, the other

10 per cent, no matter how powerful, would be obliged to take notice and act with more respect. Black economic empowerment (BEE) policies would simply formalise what is already happening. Presently, most BEE deals are characterised by a cap-in-hand role for blacks. It is an arrangement whereby blacks are accommodated as junior partners, often without any power or influence, in existing white-owned businesses. Apart from making the few blacks involved in those BEE deals wealthier, nothing else changes. That means the prospect of building a more equal society in this country in the near future is dim, to say the least.

We are one country with one economy and we should be trying to build it as such. Any attempt to build separate economies for different racial or ethnic groups would be absurd and detrimental to the common good. But there is definitely something grossly wrong when a large section of the population supports the economic ventures of another at its own cost. This tells us that the racial discrimination against and abuse of blacks will continue for as long as they are economically subservient.

The Black Consciousness Movement embarked on a journey to build an open and egalitarian society in this country, where the colour of your skin or origin would not be a point of reference. But this is not possible if blacks regard themselves as less than equal beings who enter a one-way street that will take them to a society characterised by white culture, language, mores and wealth.

I was a guest at a hotel in Livingstone in Zambia in March 2007. Noticing that almost all the African workers had white names on their name tags, I asked them for their African names. When they told me I asked why they didn't have them on their tags. They replied that they used the 'white' names to make it easier for the tourists they serve. Asked if the tourists changed their names to suit their Zambian hosts, they said, 'no'. Of course my question was rhetorical because I know whites would never do that. Whites have been living in South Africa for nearly four centuries but they don't have African names. It is Africans who give themselves white names in order to confirm their desire to be accepted by the white establishment in all its manifestations.

There was one notable exception at the hotel in Livingstone. One young black woman in the public relations unit had the African name Mweba on her name tag. She explained proudly: 'My supervisor asked me to write a white name on my tag, but I refused. I am Mweba and I will always be Mweba, and nothing else.'

Mweba has no financial muscle, but she has integrity, confidence and pride. If most blacks in our country had her attitude, we would march with greater vigour towards a truly equal and democratic society than we are doing now. And Bantu Biko, who gave his all to this country and died in service 30 years ago, would applaud.

Winifred Kgware (left), the first president of the Black People's Convention, and Mamphela Ramphele at the launch of the BPC in 1972.

Courtesy of the UWC-Robben Island Mayibuye Archives.

3. Thabo Mbeki

Steve Biko: 30 years after

Steve Bantu Biko was murdered in cold blood 30 years ago, in September 1977. The then Minister of Law and Order, Jimmy Kruger, responded to the news of this enormous crime and the death of a patriot with the infamous words: 'It leaves me cold'.

An exemplar of the racist arrogance of the regime he represented, this captain of apartheid was blind to the national and international consequences that would follow the murder of Steve Biko. The day after the murder the Chairperson of the UN Special Committee Against Apartheid, Ambassador Leslie O Harriman of Nigeria, said:

> I was shocked to learn that Mr Stephen Biko, Honorary President of the Black People's Convention and an outstanding leader of the Black Consciousness Movement in South Africa, died in detention on 12 September.

> This is one more despicable crime by the apartheid regime which has murdered a score of patriots in the past year in its police cells. It is a crime against the oppressed people of South Africa, and indeed,

against the United Nations which has proclaimed special responsibility for them. It shows that the apartheid regime is incorrigible, and that any hesitation or delay in decisive international action to enable the national liberation movement to destroy that regime is, in effect, a condonation of crimes against the patriots.

On 5 December 1977, Ambassador Harriman issued another statement in which he said:

> The judgment of the magistrate in the inquest over the death of Mr. Steve Biko is a contemptible farce which can only be enacted by the institution of apartheid. It should open the eyes of those who saw a modicum of judicial propriety in racist courts managed by racist officials under racist laws.

> I must congratulate the courageous Biko family and their able lawyers for laying bare the identity and the savagery of the murderers of Biko and their instigators and protectors. The people of South Africa and of the world have made their judgment, and the guilty men from the so-called Ministers to the Security Policemen will not escape just punishment...

> I wish to draw attention to the fact that the continued repression and acts of violence by the apartheid regime are a flagrant violation of the Security Council resolution of 29 October. The Council must take action, without any further delay, to stop its crimes. Exclusion of the apartheid regime from international organisations and from all benefits of international cooperation is the least that the international community should do.

Of great significance also is the fact that the murder of Steve Biko and the banning of Black Consciousness and other organisations spurred the UN Security Council to impose a mandatory arms embargo against apartheid South Africa on 4 November 1977. In this regard, the then Secretary General of the UN, Kurt Waldheim, said:

We have today clearly witnessed a historic occasion. The adoption of this resolution marks the first time in the 32-year history of the Organization that action has been taken under Chapter VII of the Charter against a Member State ... It is abundantly clear that the policy of apartheid as well as the measures taken by the South African Government to implement this policy are such a gross violation of human rights and so fraught with danger to international peace and security that a response commensurate with the gravity of the situation was required... Thus we enter a new and significantly different phase of the long-standing efforts of the international community to obtain redress of these grievous wrongs.

Some may ask why the murder of Steve Biko evoked such a determined international response, leading to the further isolation of the apartheid regime. Nelson Mandela provided some of the answers when he spoke in East London, on 12 September 1997, to commemorate the 20th anniversary of Biko's death. He said:

We are gathered here to pay homage to one of the greatest sons of our nation, Stephen Bantu Biko... In eulogies to the departed, the works of the living sometimes bear little relation to reality.

Yet what has been said about Steve Biko, what passed through the walls of Robben Island and other prisons along our political grapevine, has stood the test of time. That he was indeed a great man who stood head and shoulders above his peers is borne out not only by the testimony of those who knew him and worked with him, but by the fruits of his endeavours.

History called upon Steve Biko at a time when the political pulse of our people had been rendered faint by banning, imprisonment, exile, murder and banishment. Repression had swept the country clear of all visible organisation of the people. But at each turn of history, apartheid was bound to spawn resistance; it was destined to bring to life the forces that would guarantee its death.

It is the dictate of history to bring to the fore the kind of leaders who seize the moment, who cohere the wishes and aspirations of the oppressed. Such was Steve Biko, a fitting product of his time; a proud representative of the re-awakening of a people.

Where some might have understood Black Consciousness to be concerned only with the future of the black people, Steve Biko thought otherwise. It was precisely because he was a leader who understood the deep-seated humanist instincts of our people, a true representative of the re-awakening of these masses, that he could write, in 1973:

> We have set out on a quest for true humanity, and somewhere on the distant horizon we can see the glittering prize. Let us march forth with courage and determination, drawing strength from our common plight and our brotherhood. In time we shall be in a position to bestow upon South Africa the greatest gift possible – a more human face.

The Black Consciousness Movement (BCM) in our country developed during the period of extreme reaction, when both the ANC and the PAC were, like the SACP, banned organisations. This is the period of which Nelson Mandela was speaking in the quote above.

What it meant was that the ANC, the oldest liberation organisation in Africa, had reduced capacity to influence the re-awakening of the people so eminently represented by Steve Biko. We now had to confront a discontinuity in our struggle, a phenomenon that our liberation movement had never experienced before.

Early in 2001 I received a book which, among other things, discussed the BCM and demonstrated the philosophical links between it and the black consciousness movement in the United States. In an unpublished letter of thanks to the author, dated 1 April 2001, I wrote:

> Our BCM, an important part of the South African liberation movement, emerged at a time when the ANC and the PAC were banned. Consequently, for about two decades, these two organisations

could not make as direct an impact on public consciousness and mobilisation as had been the case up to 1961 and, say, after 1980.

This resulted in a 'discontinuity' that somewhat deprived the militants of the BCM of the great store of ideas and the 'political psychology' that had been accumulated by the African people during a continuous process of political struggle, certainly from the middle of the 19th century.

This, in part, explains the understandable resort to the experience and ideas of fellow Africans in America, which, naturally, will serve to elbow out the pre-BCM South African experience...

Quite correctly, the black doctors, lawyers, accountants, sociologists, educationists, economists, accountants, priests, managers, journalists and others demanded equal treatment with their white counterparts in all respects.

They also understood that these white fellow professionals had no imperative to take up this struggle for equality, as an expression of 'class solidarity', because race, fear of retribution by the apartheid state and retaining what they had to lose, including their mortgages, kept them immobilised. Accordingly, the BCM proclaimed: 'Black man you are on your own!'

Interestingly and naturally, the BCM could not exercise any significant sway over the ordinary black working people of our country. Because of many decades of struggle, these masses were already steeped in the politics of 'the Congress tradition', Congress being the African National Congress (and its allies). The ANC itself was influenced by the consciousness that had developed among these native masses as a result of their experience of white subjugation.'

These comments reflected our reading of the BCM at a certain stage of its evolution. They represented an attempt to answer questions that arose within the ANC as the BCM emerged and developed – what is this Black Consciousness Movement; what is its place in our historic struggle for national liberation; and could we count on its leaders correctly to lead the people to engage in struggle for genuine liberation?

Oliver Tambo reflected on these issues in an interview published in the Fourth Quarter 1977 edition of the ANC journal, *Sechaba*. Among other things, he said:

> In a way we started from the point of Black Consciousness too, we formed the ANC from just Africans – because the British had delivered themselves of a constitution which cut us out of power. They transferred power to the white settlers and we had to organise ourselves to defend our rights. But we have not stayed there, we have developed to the position where we expect all the people in South Africa to form part of the movement for the transformation of the social, political and economic situation. Black Consciousness, looked at from this point of view, is thus a phase in the struggle. It is not outside the struggle for human rights – on the contrary – it grows into the mainstream which has been set by the African National Congress...

> But of course there are attempts to create a movement to rival the ANC and to keep this movement different. There is talk about a Black Consciousness Movement which is not the same as the ANC and which has got somehow ultimate objectives different from those of the ANC. If there were such a group it would have no future. But, in fact, many of the leading young people who have been associated with what has been called the Black Consciousness Movement are themselves growing. They are learning politically, they are in the ANC and they have broadened their vision of the issues in South Africa. And their understanding is very clear – they are no less determined to win, not just gradual changes in South Africa, but radical immediate changes, under the banners of the ANC...

> ANC and PAC were banned. So [young people] began to react to the system and to operate politically when they had started out as civil rights organisations. SASO has begun following the same road. They started out as a body for student affairs and once they became

engaged in serious political activities they began getting arrested and persecuted. So they came closer and closer to ANC. They are legal, but their leaders are hunted down and get arrested like everyone else. And so they get to a point where they can't get any further and do what they have to do on their own. So they join the ANC.

Members of ANC in South Africa obviously can't admit that they are. When it comes to the serious question of organising and fighting, as opposed to making speeches, then they want to prepare to defend themselves and we have had many join our ranks and cease to be different after all. All these organisations that get formed: if they are innocent they are allowed to operate without their members being picked up. But if their members are seriously involved in the struggle and want to fight for their rights, the organisation is declared illegal and its members are arrested.

It is important that all of us who are seriously concerned about the true liberation of our people should understand the strategic importance of the issue of the unity of the broad movement for national liberation. In this regard, we must pay the greatest tribute to Steve Biko and his comrades in the leadership of the BCM for everything they did during a difficult moment in our struggle to defeat all efforts to divide the liberation movement.

The comments that Oliver Tambo made in this regard at the 1985 Kabwe ANC Consultative Conference remain relevant. He said:

> In our discussions, we should take all [our] historical experiences into account because, as we shall show later, the idea of a Third Force did not disappear and is still with us today. Its creation will remain a strategic objective of the forces of counter-revolution.

> In this regard, it is important to confront the matter objectively that within it our broad movement for national liberation contains both a nationalist and a socialist tendency. Our national democratic revolution has both class and national tasks which influence one another. This is natural given the nature of our society and oppression and our historical experience.

One of the outstanding features of the ANC is that it has been able to encompass both these tendencies within its ranks, on the basis of the common acceptance of the Freedom Charter as a programme that encapsulates the aspirations of our people, however varied their ideological positions might otherwise be.

The forces of counter-revolution continuously seek to separate these tendencies ('nationalist' and 'socialist' tendencies within the ANC) both politically and organisationally, set them at loggerheads and thus divide the national liberation movement. That is why the enemy always speculates about divisions between 'Marxists' and 'nationalists' within our ranks.

It is on this basis that the PAC was formed, as well as the group we have spoken of, which called itself ANC (African Nationalist). Our enemies had entertained hopes that the BCM would emerge, survive and grow as the organised representative of the 'nationalist tendency' within the national democratic revolution, independent of the ANC.

These issues are of relevance to this day particularly because certain elements within the country, which describe themselves as belonging to the Black Consciousness movement, have set themselves against the democratic movement. At the same time, significant numbers of democratic activists, particularly from among the youth, see the ANC as a socialist party and project it as such.

Though it came into being later than the period up to 1974 that we have been talking about, it might be appropriate at this stage to refer also to the formation within the ANC of a 'left' faction which dubbed itself the 'Marxist Tendency' within the ANC. This faction came out in opposition to our ally, the South African Communist Party, and sought to shift both SACTU and the ANC in a so-called left direction.

Members of this group are no longer within our ranks. It is, however, true that some of their ideas have penetrated sections of the democratic movement inside our country. These need to be combated, once more, to ensure that this movement does not splinter into left and right factions.

We cannot over-emphasise the strategic importance of ensuring the unity of the ANC, the broad democratic movement and the masses of our struggling people on the basis of our programme, our strategy and tactics. In the five-year period immediately following the Morogoro Conference, we can report that our movement achieved these objectives in the face of actual attempts to divide us.

We have already referred to the contribution that the BCM made to the activisation of our people into struggle. This is a positive contribution that we must recognise and to which we must pay tribute. We should also recognise the significant input that the BCM made towards further uniting the black oppressed masses of our country, by emphasising the commonness of their oppression and their shared destiny.

These views were built on political positions that our movement had long canvassed and fought for. Nevertheless, we must still express our appreciation of the contribution that the BCM made in this regard while recognising the limitations of this movement which saw our struggle as racial, describing the entire white population of our country as 'part of the problem.' ...

Building on what had been achieved in the past, we continued to expand our contact with the masses of our people as well as their democratic organisations, including the trade unions and the Black Consciousness Movement as well as the religious community within our country.

At this time Tambo could not comment openly on the relationship that had developed between the ANC and the BCM. During the period of extreme reaction it was important to avoid doing and saying anything that could result in leaders and activists of the BCM being arrested and charged with furthering the aims of the ANC, a banned organisation. Below, we will reflect on what, in fact, happened in the period from 1973 onwards.

In 1973, precisely to deal with those who propagated notions of 'a Black Consciousness movement which is not the same as the ANC and which has got somehow ultimate objectives different from those of the ANC', the National Executive Committee (NEC) of the ANC issued a statement defining its approach to the BCM.

Presenting the Political Report of the NEC to the Kabwe Conference, Oliver Tambo said:

> In a statement issued after its second session in 1973, the NEC said: 'In the last few years... there has come into being a number of black [consciousness] organisations whose programmes, by espousing the democratic, anti-racist positions that the ANC fights for, identify them as part of the genuine forces of the revolution.' The NEC went on to elaborate the following important positions:
>
> 'The assertion of the national identity of the oppressed black peoples is ... not an end in itself. It can be a vital force of the revolutionary action involving the masses of the people. For, it is in struggle, in the actual physical confrontation with the enemy, that the people gain a lasting confidence in their own strength and in the inevitability of final victory - it is through action that the people acquire true psychological emancipation.'
>
> Proceeding from these positions, the ANC sought to establish relations with the forces represented in the BCM and to impart to them the collective revolutionary experience of our people contained in and carried forward by our organisation. Our aim was to establish close fraternal relations with this movement and encourage it to grow, but as an instrument for the mass mobilisation of our people into struggle ...
>
> Already, the idea was beginning to emerge among some circles, particularly outside our country, that the BCM could consolidate itself as, at worst, a political formation to replace the ANC and, at least, a parallel movement enjoying the same legitimacy as the ANC.

It was of primary importance that we should deny our opponents any and both of these possibilities. Despite the severe setbacks we had suffered during the Sixties, the enemy had failed to remove the idea and prestige of the ANC from among our people.

This, together with the activities that we undertook within the country, meant that the youth whom the BCM was organising were at least conscious of the ANC, despite the fact that many had grown up without any direct contact with us. This served as a basis for us to score significant achievements in terms of building our relations with activists of the BCM and frustrating the scheme to build up a so-called Third Force.

By the beginning of 1974 a significant number of BCM refugees had arrived in Gaborone. This community of refugees and our liberation movement as a whole were brought face to face with the brutality of the apartheid regime when the outstanding SASO and BCM leader, Abram Onkgopotse Tiro, died on 4 February 1974, killed by a parcel bomb apparently posted in Geneva.

An article about and obituary for Abram Tiro appeared in Vol 8 No 4 of *Sechaba*. It reported that at the 1972 graduation ceremony at Turfloop, Tiro had said: 'Of what use will your education be if you cannot help your people in their hour of need? If your education is not linked with the struggle on the whole continent of Africa, it is meaningless.'

The article went on to say:

He was expelled the next day. Long after the world has forgotten the Vorsters, the van den Berghs and the Swanepoels, the people of our country will remember Abram Tiro, student leader and a militant against apartheid tyranny. The African National Congress of South Africa salutes the memory of this brave and courageous son of Africa and pledges to avenge his death. This and other murders of our people's heroes will not go unpunished and their memory shall ever be with us.

Coming after the benchmark 1973 ANC NEC statement on the BCM, the *Sechaba* article reflected the full acceptance of the BCM by the ANC as an authentic and integral part of the broad movement for national liberation.

Soon after Tiro's funeral in Gaborone, at which I represented the ANC, we entered into confidential discussions with another recent arrival among the BCM exiles, Sipho Buthelezi. Sipho had been sent out of the country by the BPC, led by Steve Biko, to serve as an authorised underground link between the BPC and the ANC.

Many years later, at the Kabwe Conference, Oliver Tambo publicly disclosed the message Sipho Buthelezi had conveyed to the ANC. He said:

> By this time Steve and his colleagues had arrived at the following positions: (a) That the ANC is the leader of our revolution; (b) That the Black People's Convention should concentrate on mass mobilisation; (c) That the BPC should function within the context of the broad strategy of our movement; and (d) That a meeting between the leadership of the BPC and ourselves was necessary.

These were the principal elements of the historic message communicated to us by Sipho Buthelezi. Because of the sensitivity that attached to this message, and the role that Sipho would have to play as the pivotal link between the BPC and the ANC, we had to meet him in the very early hours, while everybody else in Gaborone was asleep.

The message he conveyed also meant that we had to act immediately to elaborate the immediate steps we would have to take to give effect to the strategic partnership between the BPC and the ANC. Within this context, one of the tasks that would be undertaken by a select group within the leadership of the BPC would be to identify reliable activists within the country whom the ANC could recruit into its underground structures and Umkhonto we Sizwe.

With regard to this, Biko and other leaders of the BCM were keen that we should, at all costs, avoid the proliferation of armed formations attached to various political groups within the broad movement for national liberation.

Obviously, operations that related to the strengthening of the ANC had to be conducted with the greatest secrecy, to enable the BPC to continue its work as a legal organisation concentrating on the strategic task of mass mobilisation. Among other things, this is what necessitated that even in conditions of exile in Botswana we should keep our contact with Sipho Buthelezi very secret.

This also meant that by the beginning of 1974 Tambo and a restricted group within the leadership of the ANC fully understood that, practically, Steve Biko, Barney Pityana and others within the BCM were an integral and vital part of the leadership of our movement. From this it was clear that all attempts to separate the BCM from the ANC, putting these two movements at loggerheads, had failed dismally.

This would be confirmed in 1975, when we met leaders of SASO in Swaziland. These leaders reported that SASO had been trying since 1974 to establish a fighting partnership with the ANC similar to what had been proposed to us by the BPC leadership, and to which we had agreed. SASO was both dismayed and angry that, as far as it knew, the ANC had rejected this overture.

Fortunately, I had also been involved in the discussions in Gaborone with SASO representatives during which we had considered the possibility of the ANC and SASO establishing a strategic partnership. It was, therefore, not difficult to explain that the ANC was in complete agreement with what SASO had proposed, which coincided fully with the views of the ANC.

Immediately, therefore, at the same meeting in Swaziland, we entered into discussions with the SASO leaders about the programme of action which would give effect to the agreement to form a fighting partnership. This revolutionary partnership would protect the legal status of SASO and genuinely respect its independence, while strengthening the cohesion and effectiveness of the broad movement for national liberation on the basis of the strategic concept of unity in action and action in unity.

At some point the late Drake Koka, leader of the Black Allied Workers Union (BAWU), the trade union movement of the BCM, joined the refugees in Gaborone. Unfortunately, we were never able to establish the relationship with BAWU that we achieved with the BPC and SASO.

Nevertheless, after the 1976 Soweto Uprising, Koka was to demonstrate that his position on the leading role of the ANC in our struggle for national liberation was no different from that espoused by Biko and his comrades in the BPC and SASO.

When Tsietsi Mashinini and other leaders of the Soweto Uprising arrived in London they contacted the ANC Office and asked to meet me. I was instructed to travel from Lusaka to London to meet this group of young patriots. They informed me that they had been directed by Drake Koka to meet me and that I would give them the necessary directions about their mission now that they had gone into exile.

Unfortunately, given the high profile of the Soweto Uprising, they were persuaded by others within the international community to undertake tasks other than those we thought were appropriate. In particular, contrary to our advice, they refused to go back to school to further their studies.

As we have already indicated, and as reported by Oliver Tambo in 1985, it had also been agreed that 'a meeting between the leadership of the BPC and ourselves was necessary'. An attempt was made in 1976 to organise such a meeting between Tambo and Biko.

Botswana celebrated the tenth anniversary of its independence in 1976. Fully conscious of what the apartheid regime would think about it, the late President of Botswana, Sir Seretse Khama, invited Oliver Tambo to lead an ANC delegation to Gaborone to participate in the independence celebrations. After secret discussions with the late Beyers Naudé and others, it was decided that this would provide an opportunity to arrange a meeting between Tambo and Biko.

The plan was that a member of the Institute for Contextual Theology and close colleague of Oom Bey, and now Co-ordinator of the ANC Commission for Religious Affairs, Rev Cedric Mayson, who is also a pilot, would secretly fly Biko to Botswana from King William's Town.

Arrangements were made with the Botswana Government for the plane to land and take off on a small airstrip in the night, making it possible for Biko, then banned and restricted to King William's Town, to leave and return without this being noticed by the apartheid security forces.

In a development that was inexplicable at the time, given that very few people knew of the planned operation, on the eve of his secret flight to Botswana the South African Police mounted open and visible surveillance on Biko, making it impossible for him to fly out as arranged.

Accordingly, both the trip and the meeting in Gaborone had to be aborted. Most unfortunately, no other opportunity ever presented itself for Tambo and Biko to meet to cement the strategic partnership between the ANC and the BCM to which both these eminent leaders of our people were deeply committed.

Writing after Biko's death, and relying on her own sources, the anti-apartheid activist and writer, Mary Benson, said:

> Steve Biko, at the time of his last fatal detention, had been planning a journey in which he had hoped to meet representatives of the African National Congress and the Pan Africanist Congress of Azania to discuss with them the possibility of unity with the Black Consciousness Movement. Clearly, the security police knew of his intention, and one aim of their brutal interrogation was to discover the details of his plans. Unity of all those committed to liberation in South Africa, unity of black and black, and black and white, remains the greatest threat to the South African State.

In his report to the Kabwe Conference Oliver Tambo had said:

> This is the appropriate occasion to disclose that in the course of [our] work we had, by 1976, arrived at the point where the time had come for us to meet that leading representative of the BCM, the late Steve Biko ...Unfortunately, it proved impossible to bring Steve out of the country for this meeting. Another attempt was made in 1977 but this also did not succeed. Subsequent arrangements also failed as, for instance, Barney Pityana was arrested when he was due to lead another delegation. Steve Biko was of course subsequently murdered.

Some years later, in its submission to the Truth and Reconciliation Commission (TRC), the ANC said:

It was as a result of this interaction [with BCM representatives], over a long period, that the senior corps of BCM leadership started to co-ordinate their work with the ANC, and some of them became fully-fledged members of the underground.

The brutality against Steve Biko in detention, leading to his murder in 1977, can partly be explained by the fact that he had made moves towards contact with the ANC, and was on the verge of a historic meeting with OR Tambo. Carl Edwards and Craig Williamson knew of the link between the ANC and Biko, and they are most likely to be responsible for his betrayal. But the murderers themselves should know better, and they should shed light on this matter before this Commission.

The ANC referred to Carl Edwards and Craig Williamson because both were members of the apartheid Security Police who were in contact with Biko and the BCM. Williamson was a member of the staff of the International University Exchange Fund (IUEF), which provided scholarships to a large number of students inside and outside South Africa, and students from the rest of southern Africa, who were involved in the struggle for liberation.

The IUEF was therefore a trusted partner of the liberation movements of southern Africa, including the ANC, which enabled it to gain access to Biko and the BCM in general. We ultimately discovered that Williamson had come to learn of the plan to fly Biko to Botswana in 1976, which is what had led the SAP to mount its visible surveillance.

The fact that Williamson knew of the contact between Steve and the ANC also led the ANC to conclude that it was he and Edwards who were 'most likely to be responsible for [Steve's] betrayal' and death when the Security Police (the Special Branch) tortured him to extract information about his links with the ANC and what he knew about ANC structures in the country.

The police officers who murdered Steve Biko approached the TRC to request amnesty. Their request was denied. Undoubtedly, proceeding according to its set rules, the Amnesty Committee of the TRC refused the request because it was convinced that the killers had not told the whole truth. That truth would include the reasons why it was necessary, in the first place, to subject Steve to the intolerable and extreme violence that resulted in his death.

As Oliver Tambo said in 1985, after we failed twice to arrange for him and Steve to meet – the second meeting was scheduled to take place in Holland – it was decided that Barney Pityana would undertake this mission, after the banning in 1977 of the BCM and other organisations. But Barney was detained and held without trial for at least a year.

Once again it was Cedric Mayson who was to fly Barney out of the country. This request was conveyed to Mayson by Thenjiwe Mthintso, currently South Africa's Ambassador to Cuba. But Barney was detained, the Christian Institute was banned, and Cedric was served with banning orders.

Because of the importance that attached to the ANC-BCM meeting, ultimately Jane Phakathi was sent out of the country to meet the ANC. The meeting took place in Lusaka.

However, the situation in our country changed radically as a result of the murder of Steve, the banning of the BCM organisations, and the momentum in the struggle created by the Soweto Uprising and the growing mass movement in the country. Among other things, this led to ever-growing numbers of BCM members joining the ANC both inside and outside the country.

I feel privileged to have been asked by the President of Azapo, Mosibudi Mangena, to contribute an article to this book published to salute Stephen Bantu Biko on the occasion of the 30th anniversary of his death under the most tragic circumstances.

Having accompanied Oliver Tambo to the 1976 Botswana independence celebrations, assigned the task to receive Steve and take him to Tambo, I had looked forward to meeting Steve, if only to convey to him our appreciation of the contribution he had made and was making to the further intensification of the offensive against the apartheid regime. Unfortunately, this was not to be.

As we reflect on the indelible contribution that Steve Biko made to our struggle for national liberation, and the important place the BCM occupied in the evolving strategy of the ANC, a number of critically important matters stand out.

Firstly, Steve and his comrades took up the cudgels of struggle at a very difficult moment in our history. It required great conviction and courage, during the period of extreme reaction and repression that began with the banning of the ANC and the PAC, for Steve to elect to stand up to raise the flag of freedom in a situation in which this invited assassination by the apartheid system, as was the case with Steve, Onkgopotse Tiro, Mapetla Mohapi and other leaders of our people.

Secondly, Steve played a central and strategic role in defeating the efforts by some, fundamentally, to divide our national liberation movement by driving a wedge between the 'nationalist' and the 'socialist' tendencies in the movement. This division would have made it impossible to achieve the unity among the oppressed that was so critical to the defeat of the apartheid system and the beginning of the process of fundamental social transformation to eradicate the legacy of colonialism and apartheid.

Thirdly, this contributed enormously to reducing the possibility of the proliferation of liberation armies in our country, which might have led to confrontation and combat, as the different factions of the liberation movement sought to achieve hegemony, one over the other.

Fourthly, Steve Biko and his comrades in the BCM conducted a programme of political education that created a large cadre of revolutionaries which played a central role in the final offensive that resulted in the apartheid regime accepting the need for democratic change, a cadre that continues to play a central role in our process of reconstruction and development.

In this regard, in his speech in East London marking the 20th anniversary of Steve Biko's death, Nelson Mandela said:

> It is both natural and a matter of proud record, that the overwhelming majority of young fighters who cut their teeth and shaped part of their political being in the Black Consciousness Movement are today leaders in their own right in national and provincial government, in the public service, in the judiciary and in the security and intelligence structures of the democratic government. They are to be found in the professions, in business, in the trade union movement and other

structures of civil society – strategically placed to make their mark on the new order being born.

The attitude of mind and way of life that Biko and his comrades called for are needed today in abundance. They are relevant as we define our being as an African nation on the African continent. They are pertinent in our drive to ward off the temptation to become clones of other people.

A new attitude of mind and way of life are required in our efforts to change the human condition. But they can only thrive if we succeed in that common effort to build a better life. They are required as we strive to bring all power into the hands of the people; as we seek to shape a new media that appreciates the conditions and aspirations of the majority; as we change the structure of ownership of wealth; as we build a new ethos in our ideals, and yet at the same time, the specificity of our own concrete conditions.

While Steve Biko espoused, inspired, and promoted black pride, he never made blackness a fetish. At the end of the day, as he himself pointed out, accepting one's blackness is a critical starting point: an important foundation for engaging in struggle. Today, it must be a foundation for reconstruction and development, for a common human effort to end war, poverty, ignorance and disease.

In 1999 Steve Biko was admitted into the ranks of the National Order for Meritorious Service in Gold, which has been replaced in part by the Order of Luthuli and in part by the Order of the Baobab. Among those honoured with Steve Biko on that occasion were such outstanding patriots as Albertina Sisulu, Yusuf Dadoo, Bram Fischer, Dennis Hurley, Helen Joseph, Benny Kies, Moses Kotane, Govan Mbeki, Nthato Motlana, Lilian Ngoyi, Duma Nokwe, Robert Sobukwe, Abram Tiro, and Dr Abdurahman.

In the Solemn Oration delivered by the President of the Republic as Patron of the National Orders, the President said:

All these distinguished members of our National Orders are the guardians of *ubuntu*, handmaidens of our liberty, and defenders of a shared human destiny. They stand as beacons that must guide us forever as we build a society founded on the high ideals of freedom, justice, equality and human solidarity.

For all time, these men and women will live on as esteemed members of these Orders which constitute an affirmation of our new nationhood, as do our National Anthem, our National Flag, and our National Coat of Arms, which represent the highest symbolic repositories of our common nationhood.

The lifetime contributions of the heroes and heroines who are the principals of today's National Orders ceremony light our way as we advance to the better world that is being born.

Their footprints are the inspiring signposts that indicate our route of march, even for generations that have still to emerge out of the distant mists of future time.

We are especially blessed that this ceremony permits us to share an encounter with the honoured Members of the National Orders who live. We are especially privileged that this ceremony brings us into communion with the noble souls of the honoured Members of the National Orders who have departed from the world of the living.

To them all, the living and the dead, on this day, the nation says – *bayethe*!

On this day, let all citizens and patriots proclaim: Glory to the Honoured Members of the National Orders!

Our nation is greatly privileged that Stephen Bantu Biko is today one of the Honoured Members of the National Orders. To him the nation says – *bayethe*!

A tender moment: Biko and his younger son, Samora.

4. Darryl Accone

Through chess
I discovered Steve Biko

A world away from the dusty heat of the western suburbs of Pretoria, where I lived, in icy Reykjavik, the Cold War was reaching its apotheosis. World chess champion Boris Spassky of the Soviet Union was preparing to take on his American challenger, Bobby Fischer, in Iceland in July 1972. Through the greatest of board games (at least in the non-Asian, non-African sphere), communism and capitalism were going to clash openly through their surrogates. East versus West on 64 black-and-white squares; queens and rooks, knights and bishops standing in for the inter-continental ballistic missiles that the planet's two superpowers had pointing at each other's territory.

What came to be known as The Match of the Century exerted a profound effect on youngsters around the world and in South Africa too, even though in its 24th year of apartheid the country was increasingly cut off. Globally, tens of thousands took up the game; locally, thousands. From the start of this chess mania in South Africa, however, all was not equal. The tentacles of National Party legislation meant that chess clubs and tournaments were segregated. Whites played whites in clubs and tournaments in the cities and suburbs; blacks played blacks in township clubs and events. That age-old dichotomy of the game itself – white versus black on a flat, square, playing field of 32 black squares and 32 white squares – played out in an obverse and perverse echo in South African reality.

White chess clubs and the South African Chess Federation (SACF) woke up early to this parlous position. They declared that clubs and tournaments were open to all, an open-ended stance that did not resolve the problem. There is wishful thinking and wishful saying, and the 'open to all' declaration was redolent of both.

At the first Border Championship, from 15 to 17 December 1974, history was made. As the January 1975 issue of *The South African Chessplayer* put it: 'It was a seven round swiss open to **all** players resident in the Border area ... A pleasing feature was that among the entries were many who had never played tournament chess before, and this was the case with most of the 12 Bantu, 2 Coloured, Indian and Chinese entrants.'

Bantu. That South African pejorative arising out of misuse. That apartheid classification euphemism for race and colour, snatched from anthropology and linguistics and, most viciously of all, from the plural, in some Bantu languages, of –*ntu* (person).

Bantu. That second name in a name of South African names, Stephen Bantu Biko. Steve Biko was from the Border region, born in King William's Town on 18 December 1946 – just under 28 years before that inaugural Border chess tourney. But for a 14-year-old schoolboy in Pretoria, Steve Biko and his nom de plume, Frank Talk, were another world away. Unknown, in fact.

But through chess I discovered Steve Biko.

Like many young boys, I took up chess avidly during and after the Spassky- Fischer match. I had learnt the game six years before, but had played only against my Uncle Sid at the weekly Sunday gatherings at my grandparents' home behind their fruit, vegetable and grocery shop in Perth Road, Westdene. After the match I played and studied the game in earnest. Each month *The South African Chessplayer* would arrive with news and games from national and international tournaments.

One day an issue arrived with a banner heading across the front cover proclaiming: FIDE: WE'RE IN! The story was at the very front inside, and detailed how South Africa, having been expelled alongside Rhodesia at the 1974 Congress of the International Chess Federation (Federation Internationale Des Echecs – FIDE), had been reinstated at the 1976 Congress in Haifa, Israel.

I have that October 1976 issue still, and turning to the address given by the SACF president, Leonard Reitstein, read:

> Players of all ethnic groups can and do compete in many events organised by clubs, provincial bodies and the South African Chess Federation. To cite one recent instance, two of the competitors invited to compete in the 1975 S.A. Closed Championship were coloured. They competed in this event on merit, as did all the other competitors. Players to represent South Africa internationally will also be chosen on merit and I only hope that we will be able to prove this in the near future.

We are destined to learn and relearn that the personal is the political. By this time I had been made politically aware by many factors. There was the position of the Chinese in South Africa, stuck in a limbo, defined only by what they were not and variously classified by the National Party as non-white or coloured. There were the not-so-subtle gradations of geography and class. We had lived in Marabastad before being forced to move out of that multiracial – indeed, non-racial – Pretoria equivalent of Sophiatown to a suburb that did not really exist: Claremont. Half a kilometre from our house, the only one on a block that ran to veld on three sides, was the rubble of the late Lady Selborne, its residents long evicted and its freehold homes demolished. There were, finally, the ineluctable daily realities of apartheid, experienced in what was the military city of Pretoria, and read about in the frank reporting of the *Rand Daily Mail* that my parents and grandparents took.

South Africa's re-entry to world chess was short lived. Nine months later, at the FIDE Congress in Lucerne, the country was out once more. The difference was that Arab and Eastern bloc countries had boycotted the congress in Haifa, whereas they were back in force in Lucerne and, in solidarity with the South African anti-apartheid movement, voted to expel the SACF.

This happened despite the South African body's secret weapon: Donald Woods.

'It was decided, mainly in order to combat the political attacks we knew would confront us, to ask Donald Woods of East London to accompany us,' wrote Reitstein in the June 1977 issue of *The South African Chessplayer* (of which he was, incidentally, founder and editor).

He continued: 'Donald is, as most readers know, an active chess player and administrator, being on the Border Union and East London Club committees.'

Woods, for his part, recalled his role in a piece in the same issue. He acknowledged his mixed feelings about his self-styled mission to Lucerne, particularly that 'political enemies could make capital out of my role in the venture'. He conceded that 'the one valid indictment that I thought our opponents made was that it was not enough for our federation simply to be non-racial in attitude. We have to show that we are non-racial in practical terms in our clubs – that our chess clubs have more than a token few black players and that we are concerned about such things as the extra transport costs for chessplayers who through no fault of their own are compelled by law to live in areas far from chess clubs.'

Woods looked ahead, suggesting that 'we should set our sights on rejoining FIDE *permanently* in 1979 – *with the backing of the African federations*'. His call for action was passionate:

> To achieve African backing we would have to step up our club integration drastically. We can no longer simply proclaim that our clubs are open to all and leave it at that. Clearly we must actively pursue active recruitment in all our clubs to make our club membership as representative as possible of the South African population. For example, there are surely 'African' chessplayers in Langa, Nyanga and Guguletu – but as yet there is not one 'African' member in any Cape Town chess club. This is the sort of situation our critics rightly label as abnormal ...

... South African chess has come a long way – but it has a longer way
yet to travel. The challenge is an exciting one. I look forward to the day
when young South Africans – English, Afrikaans, 'Coloured', 'Indian',
Xhosa, Chinese, the lot will be accepted in the world chess community
so that out of their ranks can come our grandmasters of the future.

To the 17-year-old boy I was, chess crazy, all that seemed eminently
reasonable. After all, I was one of the top two schools chess players in the
Northern Transvaal (essentially, Pretoria). Still, something was wrong.
The previous year, in June 1976, protests by schoolchildren and students
had broken the complacency of my Catholic private school, or at least the
comfortable reveries of some of my fellow standard nine pupils.

And this Donald Woods had been cropping up more and more in the
papers, through his impassioned columns attacking apartheid and
advocating non-racialism in all spheres of South African life. Those
came from the East London newspaper, the *Daily Dispatch*, which he
edited, and I wondered why *The South African Chessplayer* had seemingly
neglected to mention that their Donald Woods was this Donald Woods.
This selfsame Donald Woods it was who wrote, one day, about Stephen
Bantu Biko and, because I had been won over by Woods's arguments on
chess in South Africa, I read what he had to say with care.

It must have been around the middle of August 1977. Woods was
asking what had happened to Biko, detained on 18 August under
section 6 of the Terrorism Act. Woods said he had learnt much from
Biko; that his ideas about how people could and should live together in
the country had been profoundly influenced by Biko.

A month later, the *Rand Daily Mail* reported the callous
announcement by Minister of Justice Jimmy Kruger that Biko had died as
a result of 'a hunger strike'. His later icy words chilled any sentient reader:
'I am not glad and I am not sorry about Mr Biko ... He leaves me cold,' he
told the Transvaal Congress of the National Party on 14 September, the day
after announcing Biko's 'death'. It was at this meeting that a delegate from
Springs drew appreciative laughter when he praised Kruger for allowing
Biko to exercise 'his democratic right to starve himself to death'.

All that was revealed as lies at the inquest, in Pretoria in November 1977. This was not a world away from the dusty heat of the western suburbs of Pretoria, where we lived. My family followed proceedings through the papers and were appalled at the sustained and systematic inhumanity of those questioned by Sydney Kentridge, counsel for the Biko family. Throughout the baking heat of that early summer, my matric exams took a clear back seat to the inquest. Although university beckoned, it was reduced to insignificance.

My mother wept when Kentridge exposed the three doctors – Ivor Lang, Benjamin Tucker and Colin Hersch – who confessed that they had made incorrect diagnoses. They had turned their Hippocratic oaths into hypocritical ones, she said.

It was impossible not to want to know more about Biko. Some time during my first year at university, the Heinemann African Writers Series published *I Write What I Like*, a collection of his work. The thoughts and ideology it presented did what only the best writing can: enlarged the world.

It made me wonder, too, what Biko had made of the South African chess scene and the efforts by well-meaning liberals to change it for the better. It did not seem to me that Biko would altogether have approved of Woods' general approach and particular involvement at Lucerne, in that month just before Biko was detained, tortured and murdered.

I met Donald Woods in early 1996, if memory serves. He was in Johannesburg working on a Public Broadcasting Service documentary about media freedom in the new South Africa, and for some reason I was asked to take part. Woods interviewed me at my home, and looked tired. Things were a bit rushed, so I did not ask him what I had wanted to: What did Steve Biko make of South African chess in the mid-1970s? I will never really know, with Woods dead too, but I do know that it is all too easy to judge Woods harshly, both for his bridge-building attempts in chess, and for the way that Western media and film makers have focused more on him than on Biko. (Something this essay might also be accused of doing.)

But years later, in a Winter School lecture given by Barney Pityana at the 2007 National Arts Festival, a very close approximation of the answer was afforded me. Pityana related that, invited to a South African Students' Organisation (SASO) conference in what was then Natal, he was surprised to learn that he was to be elected SASO President, as arranged by Biko. It turned out that Biko wished to concentrate on his studies, and thought Pityana's expulsion from the University of Fort Hare was a fortunate coincidence. The result was that Pityana did not take up the scholarship waiting for him at Durham University in the UK, instead staying on to share Biko's room for a year.

'He had infectious enthusiasm and loyalty to all of us,' said Pityana. 'Every issue was under debate through long nights. This was the formation of ideas. After discussions, when everyone had gone off to sleep, he would write out the results, which became the papers in *I Write What I Like*.'

Elaborating on the nature of the inquiry into the fundamentals of Black Consciousness, Pityana discussed how Biko's cadre had extended dealings with Rick Turner – later assassinated by the apartheid regime – and his acolytes, among them Halton Cheadle and Charles Nupen.

> There was a group around Rick Turner who considered themselves radicals. The discussions with them were very important. We said: 'White people cannot fight the struggle for us. The time for white liberals is gone.' As a young black group we were very clear on how whites diminished the struggle of black people. But we were still very appreciative of the intellectual discussion.

This contestation resulted in the 'main idea' of the Black Consciousness Movement: 'That it is oppressed people themselves who will be active in the struggle for their liberation.'

> We had to stop those speaking on our behalf – the liberals in parliament and the newspapers. Liberals ... could not think beyond the manifestation of evil, couldn't think that black people had a vision for the country. We said: 'Black Consciousness does not end with apartheid. It begins with it.'

How much sooner South African chess might have changed had that idea been disseminated, thought about and taken root. How different South Africa in 2007 would be if Black Consciousness provided a counterweight to the neo-liberalism that runs the country and has banished more progressive ideas of social justice.

Hope lies in new generations. In students such as those I have been privileged to teach, who have a sense of history, a sense of social justice, and a true humanity. They have those because – long before we met in the seminar room – they had been reading and thinking deeply on *I Write What I Like* by Steve Biko.

For my part, I will always be grateful to that game of white versus black, because it was through chess that I discovered Steve Biko.

Biko emerges from a police station in 1977 where Donald Woods, then Daily Dispatch *editor, is waiting to take him home. Woods had to flee South Africa in the late seventies after exposing Biko's death to the world. He died in 2001.*

Courtesy of *Daily Dispatch,* Johnnic Communications.

5.

Veli Mbele

Biko's influence on me

My early years

On 12 September 1977 when Steve Biko died I was just a year and a couple of months old, crawling around in my nappies and there was no way I could have had any inkling of some of the significant events that were unfolding around me, including the brutal death in detention of someone as iconic as Biko.

When I started my primary school education in the early 1980s everything around me seemed quite okay; not even the occasional vicious whipping from some of my teachers could tamper with my general perception of life.

The early 1980s were characterised by heightened resistance against the Boers and one image of that era will remain forever fixed in my mind: that of armed white soldiers in brown uniforms standing guard at the entrance to our school.

These soldiers were such a regular feature that I was not really bothered by their presence until we had a discussion about them and one of my classmates wanted to know why they were stationed at our school gate.

One of the older learners ventured to explain that the soldiers were there to prevent the comrades from entering our schoolyard and disrupting our lessons.

His explanation didn't make much sense to me because it was not accompanied by a thorough explanation of the general situation and, looking back, I doubt it would have made much sense even if he had given a more elaborate explanation.

After quizzing him a bit, it occurred to us that these comrades were merely learners like us except that they were at high school and they wanted us to join something known then as '*umzabalazo*' – the struggle.

At the time I was not particularly impressed with these 'comrades' because, in my mind, they were just a group of people who didn't like being in class. Therefore, in my mind, the soldiers were performing a noble act by preventing them from entering our schoolyard.

Looking back I realise that it was perhaps a good thing that I kept these thoughts to myself.

By the time I reached higher primary I began to understand a few important facts about education. I began to appreciate the importance of being present at school each day, why I had to wear uniform, and that if I didn't do my homework or disrespected my teachers or classmates there would be harsh consequences.

This did not prevent me from pulling an occasional prank or two on one of my unsuspecting classmates but it also gave birth to a new attitude – I began to see myself as a senior learner who had to behave in a particular way.

At this stage I was permitted to sit in on the sessions at which my teachers and parents scrutinised my academic performance and general conduct at school. I would sit there motionless, listening to my teachers describing me as neat, diligent, well mannered, curious, and talkative, but also as very forward and sometimes dangerously casual.

Although I did not always look forward to these sessions they afforded me the opportunity to get to know my interests better and through them I developed my fascination for history, English and biology, which later influenced my choice of subjects at high school.

My years at high school

Like most black middle-class parents my mother wanted me go to a so-called model C school, an idea that didn't appeal to me so, without informing my parents, I quietly enrolled at Tshireleco High School. My decision had very little to do with my academic interests: it was mainly influenced by the fact that, at the time, Tshireleco High was perceived to be the bastion of student struggle in our township.

Unfortunately, however, Tshireleco High had also earned the dubious title of 'Umgababa' because of its poor discipline and academic output at the time. I later learned that 'Umgababa' was the name of a popular holiday resort.

I eventually informed my parents of my decision and, surprisingly, they were not as disapproving as I had feared.

Developing consciousness

As the excitement of being a high school learner began to subside I started to interact with my books in earnest and, while doing so, discovered that there was something uncanny about the history books.

In them, people of European descent such as Garibaldi, Napoleon and Bismarck were portrayed as great and intelligent leaders, while most black leaders were just savages who were killing each other.

This raised many questions in my mind and, in my quest for answers, I, together with some of my classmates, decided to ask the teacher a few searching questions.

After reviewing our first engagement with our history teacher we realised our approach would not yield the desired results and we decided that after school we would spend two hours in the local libraries searching for answers to some of the questions our teachers were reluctant to answer.

The practice of doing extra research after school proved so beneficial to our intellectual and academic development that we constituted ourselves into a formal group to investigate and inform young African people about issues relating to African history, religion, philosophy and politics.

So, in 1992, we formed the Africa Youth Movement (AYM). At the time of its formation, the AYM didn't define itself along strict political lines because we were of the view that politics was a trade for the less trustworthy and that authentic material on African history was very hard to come by so the available material had to be treated with considerable suspicion.

As part of the AYM's programme, we had regular internal debates on Africanism, Black nationalism, Black theology, Zionism and many other topics. We would dissect the Bible, the Quran and the works of Ali Mazrui, Cheik Anta Diop, Marcus Garvey, Ahmed Deedat and other influential African scholars.

The material we studied radically altered our outlook on the world, including our views on creation, God, religion, history and culture and, because of this new-found consciousness, the AYM became the first forum through which I began to interrogate my existence and my being.

Our group engaged in fierce debates with other youth groups, like Alkebulan, which had a similar outlook and, as a result, we became a force to be reckoned with in the local student movement and began to attract the attention of a variety of youth groups.

One such group was the Congress of South African Students (Cosas), which, at the time, dominated most of the political activity at our school and was affiliated to the African National Congress (ANC).

We also attracted the attention of the Azanian Students' Movement (Azasm), which was affiliated to the Azanian People's Organisation (Azapo) and which, at the time, had no branch at our school.

As part of our study of the various political ideologies and philosophies that characterise the African continent we studied the ideological and political outlook of the ANC, the Pan Africanist Congress (PAC) and the Black Consciousness Movement (BCM). Because of our own orientation we found ourselves more attracted to Azasm, although we were very discreet about it.

What made the other groups unattractive was the fact that they viewed our distinctiveness as a threat and even attempted to intimidate us out of existence, but we stood our ground. As a result, after week of intense meetings and consultation we ultimately decided to align ourselves with Azasm. It was not an easy decision because we realised we were entering the terrain of politics and we were not very trusting of political organisations. We therefore decided not to disband the AYM until we were certain we could advance our mission through Azasm.

My early years in the BCM

In our area Azasm was not as organised as we had initially thought, but we realised we had much in common with the organisation although it was primarily a national student organisation with political leanings and, for the AYM, politics was really only a subject for debate.

After going through some the basic documents of Azasm we consulted with some of its local leaders – among them Tebogo Maarman, Hlangulani Mpikwane and Aslam Tawana, all of whom were very polite, intellectually sharp and highly articulate. Our meetings gave us an opportunity to get to know them personally and our continuous engagement with them developed into friendship.

My particular friend was Aslam Tawana, an interesting character – engaging and eloquent, with a sharp voice and, sometimes, a very boisterous manner, which made people who did not know him well uneasy. But this didn't stop us from becoming very good friends.

We became comfortable in our new-found home and saw no need to disband the AYM because it had effectively dissolved into Azasm. Our decision was mainly influenced by what we understood Black Consciousness to mean in the context of black history, culture, philosophy and politics.

So, in 1993, we formed the first branch of Azasm at Tshireleco High and I became the founding chairperson and later served as deputy president and president of the Students' Representative Council (SRC) in the same school in 1994 and 1995 respectively.

Our decision to join and expand Azasm challenged the dominance of Cosas and it immediately became clear to us that Cosas was not going to make it easy for us to operate, but we were prepared for this reaction.

The rise of Azasm at our school and its ultimate domination of the space previously occupied by Cosas naturally generated considerable political tension, which, fortunately, did not escalate to the point of physical confrontation.

My involvement in Azasm not only moulded me as a young leader it also prepared me for bigger roles in the community. Through Azasm we formed cultural and other organisations. Some of our most significant activities were our campaigns against gang violence and our promotion of the progressive 'Save Black Education' campaign, whose popular manifestation was the 'Employ Black Teachers' campaign.

Azasm also prepared me for larger leadership roles in other BCM structures. When I finished high school in 1995 I went on to further my studies at the then Free State Technikon, where I was received by Lesego Mogotsi, Selaocwe Kabelo, Zongezile Vena and Zola Ndaliso, who were the more experienced leaders of Azasco.

The Azasco I encountered at the Free State Technikon was not the dominant force I had imagined it to be. Fresh from Azasm, which was setting the country alight at the time, I felt Azasco to be somewhat politically timid.

Despite this I involved myself actively in its programmes and later became branch chairperson but could not complete my studies because of the unfavourable political climate on campus.

Despite the fact that the 1994 general election had taken place, the situation at the Free State Technikon did not favour black students and, given the choice between joining the growing chorus of amorphous rainbowism or standing up and defending the dignity of black students, we naturally opted for the latter option.

Our stance intensified the confrontations between black and white students and, not surprisingly, given the degree of collusion between some members of the Technikon's management and the local police, black students were always the ones who were arrested. We also understood that we were in the 'Orange Vrystaat' and in this part of our country the Boers were not in the business of making life easy for blacks.

In 1997 I moved to the Western Cape and enrolled in the Peninsula Technikon, where I was received by Tebogo Mohajane and Mendo Ramncwana, members of the branch leadership. At the time this branch of Azasco had been suspended by the SRC, who were of the view that Azasco's membership policy, which stated that 'membership shall be open to black students only', was racist and exclusionary.

The SRC's interpretation of this policy was erroneous because, since its inception, the BCM's definition of black addressed itself to the sociopolitical condition of the blacks and the role blacks must assume in the struggle to extricate themselves from oppression.

There was no reference to race or skin colour in this definition and therefore, there was absolutely nothing racist or exclusionary about it. But we knew the real motive behind the suspension of Azasco was the fact the SRC was afraid to recognise the organisation because, if Azasco were allowed to operate freely, it might radically change the balance of power in the student body.

The University of the Western Cape branch of Azasco continued to support our branch and, with the help of some of its more experienced leaders like Nelvis Qekema, Chris Swepu, Sithembiso Pakade and many others, in May 1998 the suspension of Azasco was unanimously annulled by the SRC Annual General Meeting.

This victory left the SRC highly embarrassed and paved the way for the rise and dominance of Azasco at the Peninsula Technikon during that era.

After serving as branch chairperson I went on to lead the Western Cape region and, in 1998, I was elected National Deputy President of Azasco. After suspending my studies for a brief period I resumed studying and was elected National President of Azasco in April 2003.

When I left the Peninsula Technikon I continued my involvement in BCM structures and was appointed to the national leadership of Azapo in 2004 as Deputy Secretary for Political Education and later as Deputy Secretary for Education and Culture. In September 2006 I was elected to the Standing Committee of Azapo as Secretary of Youth, a position I still hold.

When I joined the Black Consciousness Movement I was only 16. At the time the environment was not entirely friendly towards the BCM and socially many other things were yearning to devour me, but I was too immersed in the work of Azasm.

Our belief in Black Consciousness was so strong we were not prepared to go into hiding purely because other forces had threatened to 'deal' with us or deny us employment if we didn't abandon our political beliefs. This kind of reaction fortified us even more and we decided to spread the gospel of Black Consciousness even more vigorously.

Apart from political thuggery, as young people we also had to deal with a number of other personal challenges and, when I look back, I cannot imagine how many of my political peers would have survived the turbulence of township and university life without the teachings of Black Consciousness.

The only time I recognised the danger to which we were exposing ourselves was when I sat down to discuss some of my thoughts with my mother.

Looking back, I now realise how right she was when she warned that our involvement could get us killed and we must be careful as we went about our business.

Our resolve to continue with what we were doing was informed by what Black Consciousness had taught us: that it was the mission of the 'system' for us to kill one another so that white people could continue to dominate us. But we were also driven by the conviction that one can't call oneself a 'tower' but continue to be indifferent to the plight of one's own people.

The impact of Black Consciousness on me

I grew up in an environment in which many of my peers did not value their own lives and I consider myself fortunate to have encountered Black Consciousness at an early stage. Black Consciousness helped to transform my self-concept and self-esteem in a remarkable way.

My own parents barely spoke my home language, isiZulu, and because of the limited number of Nguni schools in our township I had to do all my primary and secondary schooling in isiXhosa. This presented me with serious self-esteem and identity challenges, especially when I had to interact with young people from other parts of our country, who, unlike me, had the benefit of being raised in environments where they used the same language at home and at school.

As the teachings of Black Consciousness began to take root in my head I started on a lonely and intriguing journey to discover and learn my language and culture. This not only clarified my cultural roots, it also increased my self-esteem and gave my life greater meaning and purpose.

Black Consciousness made me realise that my education was worthless if I could not use it to extricate my community from the vice of poverty, violence, disease and ignorance. It instilled in me the urge to want always to serve my community and not to expect any special recognition or reward for doing so.

Thanks to Black Consciousness many in my generation were transformed into disciplined young black men who, through their community activism, earned the respect and admiration of their peers, families and the community.

Ever since I came into contact with Black Consciousness I have felt complete, content with who I am and, most importantly, that I'm worthy of respect and dignity. As we mark the 30th anniversary of the death of Steve Biko I sincerely hope that all those who have been touched by Biko's ideas will play their part in ensuring that we expose as many young black people as possible to the teachings of Black Consciousness. In all sincerity I can't imagine how many of them will survive the social turbulence of life in South Africa today without constant doses of Black Consciousness.

A smartly-dressed Biko poses for a photo before getting into a car.

Courtesy of *Daily Dispatch*, Johnnic Communications.

6.

Mandla Seleoane

Biko's influence and a reflection

Introduction

Publishing essays in memory of Steve Biko is not only a fitting way of commemorating the 30th anniversary of his cruel murder, it is also evidence of how not even death has been able to curtail his influence.

I am grateful to have been invited to contribute an essay to this project, and to be afforded an opportunity to bear testimony, along with others, about how Steve touched my life. Because I have been requested to write about Steve's impact on a specific aspect of my life I have to speak about myself, which is not a comfortable thing to do. Hopefully the reader will focus on what Steve did for me and see that this essay is about him and not me.

To understand what Steve did for me you have to see me before I was exposed to him.

Background

I grew up in Middelburg in what was then the Transvaal (now Gauteng). Although we never had to worry about where our next meal would come from, we were not well-to-do. My father drove one of those little Ford Prefect cars. Our horizons did not allow us to imagine that an ordinary car might have a transmission system with four forward gears, let alone six!

My father's little jalopy was wont to jump every now and then out of top gear into neutral. To get its transmission system to function properly would have set the family budget back a few months. So my father's solution to the problem was very practical: once you reached driving, as opposed to accelerating, speed (not that the difference was always perceptible!), you simply kept one hand on the steering wheel and the other on the gear lever to ensure the car stayed in top gear.

This was not the only problem we had with my old man's car. My parents came from Herschel in the Eastern Cape. Often when they were on leave they would bundle all six of us kids up and throw us into the Ford Prefect and take us on an enjoyable long drive to Herschel. I still drive there every once in a while to stay connected with my ancestral roots. I just can't believe that I make the trip in so much less time!

Every now and then when the road became a little too steep our adorable jalopy couldn't make it to the top. Here again my father had a practical solution: he had figured out that in reverse gear the old Prefect would negotiate just about any gradient. But if road conditions did not allow the old man to reverse up he would drop us off just before the steep bit started, approach it as fast as he could, and wait for us on the other side.

My father, a South African Railways and Harbours policeman, always cycled to work even when he had a car. I came to discover that on the rare occasions that he used the car to go to work he would park it far from the station and walk the remaining distance. Trying to understand this rather bizarre behaviour I eventually found the courage to ask him to explain himself to me – when I was a child you needed courage to suggest even remotely that your old man was doing something that called for an explanation!

He told me that if his white superiors at work were ever to discover that he had a car they would be very unpleasant to him. I did not understand why my father was concerned about what his white superiors might think. He had acquired the car through the sweat of his brow and it was really none of their business.

In those days we had municipal police in various townships: black jacks, we used to call them because they wore black uniforms. One of my father's superiors was one Sergeant Myburgh. He was very fond of his drink and every black person at the Middelburg railway station called him (out of his hearing, of course) *kaffirtjie* (little kaffir), which was how he referred to black people. One Sunday afternoon our peace was disturbed by a loud knock on the door and Myburgh's voice, calling for my father. Hot in pursuit were the black jacks – white people were not ordinarily allowed to enter the township. This, needless to say, was more for their protection than ours. The black jacks were followed by the South African Police, who had got wind that they were trying to arrest a white man and had pursued them in order to prevent the sacrilege.

When the SAPs arrived they had very little interest in the black jacks: their concern was the whereabouts of the boss man. Myburgh emerged from our house fairly nonchalantly and explained that he was a police officer and was in the township in order to see his 'kaffir policeman'. The SAP demanded to know who his 'kaffir policeman' was and he called out to my father, who had little choice but to present himself and confirm that he was the person Myburgh had come to see.

After they had left, my father was seething with anger that Myburgh had called him a kaffir policeman in front of his children, his wife and the black jacks – in that order. I did not understand why he waited till Myburgh had left before venting his anger. My father's conduct, from parking his car far from his workplace in order to avoid offending the likes of Myburgh, through to keeping his peace when insulted, only to express his anger after the offender had left, did not make a lot of sense to me.

What compounded my difficulty was that I knew he was a fighter. Indeed, before the arrival of the SAP he had dared half a dozen black jacks to enter his house in pursuit of Myburgh. I accepted that perhaps I would never understand my father, but hoped that I might one day have a decent job, buy him a better car, and perhaps even make it unnecessary for him to work with the likes of Myburgh. I set my sights on becoming a lawyer and immersed myself in my schoolwork in the hopes that I might one day realise my dreams.

Making sense of social injustice

My father's work entailed, among other things, ensuring that people did not sell goods on trains without a licence. I never really understood why there was something wrong with people selling things they had acquired by honest means, if they also paid to be on board the train.

However, I came to understand that not only in trains but everywhere in South Africa the police chased people who sold things without a licence in order to make a living. Running from the police – often abandoning your hard-earned stock – was the natural order of things. Then I read a story in the *Rand Daily Mail* about some 'cheeky' university students, who not only refused to run when the police approached, but also refused to surrender their merchandise!

The scene was Park Station in Johannesburg. The students were members of the South African Students Organisation (SASO). Their merchandise was SASO newsletters. The year, as I recall, was 1969. SASO had been launched at the University of the North earlier that year, with Steve Biko as its president. Father Aelred Stubbs in later years remarked, talking about Steve's bravery, that 'courage is infectious' and it seems to me that evidence of the infectiousness of Steve's moral and physical courage had already emerged in 1969, an era when it took a great deal of courage for young black people to be defiant in the face of an almighty police force. Until then, the mere appearance of members of the police was enough to instil fear in the hearts of black people.

I have memories of long queues of black people in different parts of the country being marched to a distant police station, without handcuffs, by a single policeman, armed only, if at all, with a baton, and never even thinking of escaping. So the fact that these students stood their ground and were articulate in putting their case, first about why they would not run and then about their right to sell the SASO newsletter was, for me, quite a liberating moment. From that point I made it my business to read as much as I could about these 'Black Power' people, as they came to be called.

Giving me tools to understand things that befuddled me

My first impressions of the world of work were formed at home and framed by the experiences of my parents, more particularly, my father.

I knew a few white people who made a living by selling expensive clothes and beautiful fabrics. We called them travellers because they came mostly from Johannesburg and travelled around the countryside selling their wares door-to-door. My parents were regular clients of these guys. My father never asked them to produce a licence before buying from them, and I never saw them take to their heels at the sight of the police. Perhaps they did have a licence, but I could not understand why nobody even asked.

Steve provided me with a handle to try and understand what the issue was. He argued in 'Black Consciousness and the Quest For a True Humanity' that none of the things I agonised about – and believed were almost natural – were the work of God. They were, all of them, called forth by human beings who were searching for wealth, comfort and power. They could not succeed in their plans if they did not so arrange things that we black people came to see what was happening to us as the natural order of things, 'the South African way of life'. Our acquiescence in what was happening in South Africa was very much part of the grand design.

He spoke and wrote about how white folk, in order to justify our economic exploitation, originally introduced the lie that black people were inferior, and how the lie had developed an internal logic of its own until not only white folk, but indeed we, too, came to believe it. The result of us internalising this lie was that we came to negate everything that was black and strove to emulate white people. I remember, indeed, how, when I did something my mother was proud of she would say: '*umlung' omnyama!*' (a black white man), indicating that what I had done, and what she was so proud of, could not ordinarily be expected from a black person.

Steve argued that in order to work seriously for our place in the sun we ought to accept that God, or whoever was responsible for our existence, had not made a mistake in making us what we were.

In later years I, of course, learnt that the ideas Steve was putting forward were not completely new – others, notably Paolo Frere and Frantz Fanon, had already made those points way before the birth of SASO. Nonetheless, for me Steve, not Frere or Fanon, was the liberator because I heard and read him long before I knew anything about them. I recognise the pioneering work they did in uncovering us to ourselves and possibly to Steve, but I came to know and understand myself and my place in the world through Steve.

My parents' experiences at work, and the incomprehensible manner in which they responded to them, forced me to think critically about the world of work at an early age. Steve gave me the initial framework for understanding the unequal relationship that made my father come forward when the SAP demanded to know who Myburgh's 'kaffir policeman' was, and present himself as such, then seethe with anger after all the offenders had left. He provided me with the lens through which I was to view and understand our almost automatic acceptance that white hawkers were kosher, when we were planting all manner of obstacles in the way of black hawkers: we had internalised the prejudices of white folk against us and were projecting them back.

Steve argued that South Africa had made economic progress through the cheap labour provided by black people. Black workers, however, did not seem to appreciate or understand fully their contribution to making the country what it was. Black workers had to bargain with employers for a meaningful share in the profit they helped create, but they would never do that significantly until they understood their central place in creating that profit.

For a good number of us these words were not too difficult to identify with. We came, many of us, from working class backgrounds. Our parents woke up early in the morning to go to work and returned home late. As Malcolm X might have said, they worked from can't see to can't see. They hardly had any time to raise us, and it must remain a miracle, as Steve once observed, that any child in our circumstances grew to adulthood. Yet the harder our parents worked, the less they had to show for it.

So, when Steve analysed relations in the workplace he spoke about our lived experience. If, in subsequent years, I was able to follow the writings of Adam Smith, Karl Marx, Vladimir Lenin, Leon Trotsky and others on the problems thrown up by the reality of one person working for another, it was largely because Steve had already helped me understand the tension between my father and Myburgh. Steve had already predisposed me to work among employed people, trying to raise their awareness about the issues and to encourage them to tackle them.

Me and the world of work

Steve wrote the following in 'Black Consciousness and the Quest For a True Humanity':

> The system concedes nothing without demand, for it formulates its
> very method of operation on the basis that the ignorant will learn...
> the child will grow into an adult and therefore demands will begin to
> be made. It gears itself to resist demands in whatever way it sees fit.
> When you refuse to make these demands, and choose to come to the
> round table to beg for your deliverance, you are asking for the
> contempt of those who have power over you.

What I learned earlier on from Steve in the context of the employment situation was that we deal with a contradictory relationship. The employer gains more profit the less it pays the employee in wages. One must obviously concede that not all employment relationships are exploitative in that sense. It remains true, however, that even in employment relationships that are not exploitative those who are higher up in the organisation tend to be paid much better than those who are lower down. I would go so far, indeed, as to argue that it is possible to pay those who are higher up so handsomely precisely because it is possible to pay those who are lower down so miserably.

I learned, initially from Steve, that the employee must learn to demand a bigger share in the profits made as a result of his/her labour. I learned that even in an organisation that is not, by nature, exploitative employees might have to make demands to which those in charge will not easily concede. These demands will be resisted because they will reduce the profitability of the organisation. They will be resisted because they are in conflict with the high remuneration levels of the top brass.

That should not deter the employee from making the demands, for only in that way will he/she progress in life. Not making demands was not, and remains not, an option. Despite the fact that the system was designed precisely to pre-empt and resist the demands it did not respect one for not making them. Indeed, I learned from Steve that in the privacy of his heart the oppressor must have more respect for those who fight him than for those who readily present themselves for his scorn! How else could it be?

It was necessary, if one was to be the conveyer of this message, that one believe it oneself. If in one's own life one approached those in authority cap-in-hand, one would discredit the message one had to deliver.

So, Steve's message was as much a challenge to me in my working life as it was to convey it to others. I was and remain unable to deal with my bosses on a cap-in-hand basis, a factor that has proved and continues to prove costly, for I was unable to hold down any job for longer than a few months. Indeed, one job I could not hold down even for one day. Perhaps some detail will not be altogether out of place.

The narrative goes back to 1972, shortly after the strikes at black universities, following the expulsion of Onkgopotse Tiro from Turfloop. Gladwyne Melato and I had been expelled, along with other students, from Turfloop and had landed ourselves clerical jobs at the Arnot Power Station. We were a little too much for the station manager but his mild liberal tendencies made it difficult for him to fire us. However, they did not prevent him from ensuring that in the end we were fired, as long as he could, like Pontius Pilate, wash his hands of the thing.

After about three months at the station he decided to 'transfer' us to

Hendrina, where the manager was an incorrigible racist. He arranged for us to be transported to Hendrina and, on arrival, we were inducted into the Hendrina way of doing things. Among others things we were told that the manager did not speak English to black people – in fact he detested black people who addressed him in English. In order to avoid any misunderstanding on this very important issue the practice was that all black people, regardless of their station, must speak to the manager through an interpreter. They speak in their vernacular and a fellow black employee, the *induna* (head clerk, as it were), translates the employees, words into Afrikaans.

The other important piece of information we should have as newcomers was that the manager might come into our office – clerks shared a huge open space – any number of times in a day and that every time he came in we had to stand up and greet him. Gladwyne and I thought it wise not to unpack our cases as it was already very clear that we would not spend more than one night at the station.

When morning came we readied ourselves, in a manner of speaking, for Armageddon. As part of the preparation for the showdown we bought ourselves newspapers – we had been advised the previous evening that one of the things the manager hated most was a black person reading a newspaper during work hours. The big boss came in and everyone shot to their feet except Gladwyne and me. He paced around restlessly, clapping his hands as if to draw our attention to what everyone else had done when he entered. We had our attention firmly buried in the newspapers until he went out.

The boss sent for us, saying we were to come immediately. We asked the *induna* to tell him we would be there in a while, we first needed to answer the call of nature. Gladwyne took a little longer and when he eventually came into the boss's office I was locked in an argument with the *induna*, who was insisting that I should greet the boss although I had, on entering, said 'good morning Sir'. Gladwyne strolled in, still zipping up. That was like the ultimate insult, and the boss man ordered a truck immediately to drop us off in Middelburg, from where we could find our way back home.

That was the first price we had to pay in the world of work for the teachings of Steve. It would not be the last. Middelburg was, and remains, a small town. It was very hard to attract the attention of the security police without prospective employers knowing about one and eventually just about every employer in town knew that employing me was only asking for trouble. It was not long, therefore, before I became completely unemployable in Middelburg.

When I was young my parents must have hoped that one day I might be the agent through which they might be introduced to a better life. Indeed, many good parents in those days endured hardships in their workplaces in the hope that if their children got some education they might lead the dignified life in their old age that they were not afforded during their working life. And yes, many a parent took the view that it was necessary to endure these hardships so their offspring might live a better life.

It was, therefore, a sad blow to my parents when I was not only expelled from university but refused to return when I could. The least they could expect in the circumstances was that I would work and help the family. Being unemployable because of political views and aspirations, the realisation of which was a far-fetched dream was, for them, outrageous! Not only had I failed them in their hope that I might one day help them enjoy a better life I would clearly, myself, never have the life that they had hoped I might; the life they had allowed themselves to be subjected to indignity in order to create for me. Everything had simply been a waste!

The fact that I was unemployable was difficult for me too. In addition, I felt that I had betrayed my parents. They really should not have invested any money at all in my education if all it would produce was an unemployable young man! Many times I came very close to giving up, but every time I would hear Steve's words, almost like the secret voice that troubled Socrates whenever he was about to make a wrong decision:

We have set out on a quest for true humanity, and somewhere on the distant horizon we can see the glittering prize. Let us march forth with courage and determination, drawing strength from our plight and our brotherhood [we can add sisterhood too!]. In time we shall be in a position to bestow upon South Africa the greatest gift possible – a more humane face.

The horizon was distant, quite literally. The vision of the glittering prize was blurred most of the time, but very compelling precisely for that reason. I reasoned that if my parents had done a little more towards its realisation it might not be quite so distant, and the vision might be a little clearer. As much as I appreciated my parents' views and feelings I did not wish my children to feel the same about me. And so, I resolved to live with the fact that I was unemployable, with all the tensions it implied between things once hoped for and current realities, and work towards a South Africa with a more humane face.

If anything was clear to me, it was if our forebears had put their shoulders to the wheel, the load my parents carried, which gave me so much pain, might have been much lighter. It was also clear that neither my parents nor my children would be better off unless we gave South Africa the face that Steve implored us to.

So I did what I could to work towards that, wherever I found myself. Whether it was doing research for the Surplus People's Project on forced removals or for the University of Cape Town on the conditions of farm workers or hostel dwellers, writing social studies course materials for the South African Council for Higher Education (SACHED), training trade unionists and priests on labour issues or helping debunk the myth that black mineworkers could not hold blasting certificates, working as an education officer for the Commercial, Catering & Allied Workers Union or producing the *Azanian Labour Journal*, my hope and my desire was to work towards the South Africa Steve had lived and died to achieve.

Conclusion

In the end I never got to be the lawyer I had hoped to become. I have no regrets about that. If I had succeeded in becoming that lawyer I hope

I would have served the cause of liberation just as well, although that was not part of my calculations when I decided to study law. I sometimes feel, however, that making money might be a distraction from social causes.

Thirty years after his brutal murder, are we anywhere near giving South Africa the humane face that Steve spoke about; a postulation which anchored and held me in check during stormy historical moments? I think that depends on how that humane face is defined. Some may say that the dispensation we have in South Africa today is precisely the one Steve spoke about. Others might say it is only a step on the way to achieving it.

I recognise that it is important that we have formally dismantled apartheid in South Africa but I do not always know that we are, therefore, on the way to giving the country a more humane face. I am even less convinced about the proposition that we have arrived at the place to which Steve pointed.

Steve, as I have suggested, thought that racism was an ideological construct. In his view, it had a very definite and practical use. It allowed white people to go to bed and be at peace with themselves in the face of the untold atrocities they were inflicting on fellow human beings. Steve appears to me to have made a perfectly valid point, for hear the words of that celebrated French philosopher, Montesquieu: 'It is not possible for us to think that slaves are human beings, because if we acknowledge that they are human beings then we must begin to suspect that we ourselves do not behave like Christians.'

Steve acknowledged that, in time, racism became a problem in its own right; that it developed a logic of its own, separate from and independent of the purpose it was introduced to serve. Therefore he conceded that many white people actually honestly believe that black people are inferior. He understood further that black people had, themselves, come around to believing in their own inferiority.

The removal of the basis for white and black people believing that blackness spells inferiority is one of the things that, in Steve's view, we would need to achieve in order to attain the humanity he sought.

I do not know if we have succeeded in doing that in South Africa today. I still see evidence of intelligent black people looking to white people for validation. I still see evidence of intelligent black people believing that not much of value can come from other black people. Perhaps they are right, and perhaps they are wrong. Whichever way we look at it, the conclusion must be the same: we are as far today from the South Africa Steve pointed us to, at least on this question, as we were when he uttered those words more than 30 years ago.

Steve recognised racism as being secondary to economic exploitation. It must follow that one of the things we have to work towards if we hope to bestow a more humane face on the country is a dispensation that begins to introduce economic justice. If we have not succeeded in weeding out racism from the South African body politic our achievements are even less spectacular in the area of introducing economic justice.

Even more tellingly, Steve envisaged a society in which we might all be brothers and sisters. Another way of stating this would be to say that Steve hoped that somewhere on the distant horizon we might overcome hatred for one another and live in peace, harmony and security. It does not matter, in the final analysis, how successful we are in any other respect. If we continue to butcher one another in the manner that we do, South Africa's face will carry ugly scars that can never be reconciled with the society Steve lived and died to achieve.

I can still hear Steve's voice from the distant horizon whenever an injustice is committed against a fellow human being: 'In time we shall be in a position to bestow upon South Africa the greatest gift possible – a more humane face.'

I hear his voice the more clearly when black people commit the injustice, for that is not only a betrayal of a principle Steve lived and died for but also a sad reminder of the long journey we still have to travel.

BPC colleagues carry Biko's corpse to a private mortuary in King William's Town in September 1977 after having expressed their distrust of the government's post mortem.

Pallbearers take Biko to his final resting place in King William's Town, 25 September 1977. Father Drake Tshenkeng (front left), then executive member, and Hlaku Rachidi (front right), then president of the BPC.

7. Bokwe Mafuna

The impact of
Steve Biko on my life

It is quite clear to me that had I never met Steve Biko my life would have taken a completely different course. We met at a time when I had been looking for answers to the challenges facing black people under apartheid. He helped me to find some of those answers to guide me on my route towards liberating myself from racial, mental and spiritual oppression, degradation and exploitation.

I was not the only one searching for higher truths, I belonged to a group of black political soulmates who had discovered other soulmates across the seas, in America – Eldridge Cleaver, Bobby Seal, Huey Newton, and Angela Davis, Malcolm X and Martin Luther King who fought for the rights of black people, and singers Nina Simone and Aretha Franklin who sang heart-rendingly about the suffering and pain of black people. But they were all far away and we could only meet them in records and in books stolen from the Campus Bookshop near Wits University, which none of us was attending; or the Vanguard Bookshop in the city. We yearned for local heroes. But in the early sixties the apartheid regime had banned, imprisoned and banished men and women who might have played that role and forced others into exile.

Both the African National Congress (ANC) and its rival sister movement, the Pan Africanist Congress (PAC) had been banned, the South African Communist Party (SACP) had been outlawed and the South African Indian Congress (SAIC) was dysfunctional. All we knew and heard of were apartheid government policies and the Bantustan structures and their stooge leaders.

Most of us were living in the black township of Alexandra township (Alex to the locals or Dark City for having no electricity). We would meet at 67 Second Avenue, where I had a small two-roomed house, including a darkroom. I had become a photographer after leaving the trade union movement in protest against government policies, which the Trade Union Council of SA (TUCSA) wanted to adopt. I was secretary general of the Engineering Workers Union, which was dismissed from the federation, a decision that ultimately led to South Africa itself being dismissed from the International Labour Organisation.

Our group included people like Montshiwa Moroka and Moji Mokone from Diepkloof. From Alex came Mongane Wally Serote, the poet and novelist; Frank Nkonyane and his brother Madoda; Gideon Serote, Wally's half-brother; Thami Mnyele, the artist who was assassinated by the South African Defence Force in its raid on Gaborone, Botswana in 1985; Vukile 'Outlaw' Mthetwa, who was studying law at Ngoye at the time; and Skwizi Sethshedi, a very angry young black man.

Then there was Cindy Ramarumo, the only woman in our group – and still one of my dearest friends. It was Cindy who, later, would introduce me to my wife, Khayo.

It was 1969 and I had not yet heard of Steve Biko or the South African Students' Organisation (SASO), the movement he was organising and which was to play a crucial role in the struggle against apartheid. It was Cindy who first came into contact with Biko at the University of Natal (Black section) medical school. She had been invited there by Mamphela Ramphele, a fellow student and close friend of Steve's.

When Cindy came back to Alex she was excited. She told us that she had met people who talked exactly like ourselves, and who read the same books, listened to the same music – and were organised! We, on

78

the other hand, were angry and bitter; we were not prepared to take any nonsense from any white man, or woman, even – and especially – policemen, whom we described as pigs. But organised we certainly were not. So, meeting one of these students became a dream.

Unlike many of my friends I had never set foot in a university and, though I was acquainted with the work of writers like Frantz Fanon, the black revolutionary thinker from Martinique and Frederick Douglass, a black American writer who in the 1800s escaped from slavery and urged fellow slaves to do likewise. About the works of Marx, Engels, Lenin, Stalin and Trotsky I knew nothing.

Had I not met Steve at that juncture in my life I don't believe I would have gone into exile later, and would probably have ended up working steadily and drinking heavily as a journalist. I went into journalism as a direct result of our anger at the white people we visited to enjoy their drinks, snacks and, occasionally, their mates. It was a great thing – and a curious contradiction in those days – to become involved with white women. They seemed equally to relish the excitement and the adventure. Oh Fanon, where were you?

We were tired of attending white parties and being asked about what was happening in the black townships and communities. We were tired of being regarded as 'a window on the townships', through which the white man could peep and 'see how they [the darkies] live'. We were equally exasperated by black journalists and reporters who were not telling it like it is. Our group decided we must become our own voice and not let others do the talking for us or, worse, misrepresent our point of view.

That is how I came to work on the *Rand Daily Mail*, which was regarded as a prestigious liberal newspaper, its leaders a constant challenge to apartheid. I was taken on through the intervention of the newspaper's political correspondent, Jill Chisholm, whom I had met during my trade union days. I worked as a freelancer for what was known as the Township section of the paper under the supervision of Peter Wellman, a good journalist if ever there was one!

The Township section dealt exclusively with news from and about black people. Apart from Peter, all of us in that section were black.

That was the *Rand Daily Mail* at its best. It was during this period that Peter invited me to attend a cocktail party somewhere in the white suburbs. He mentioned that Biko might be there together with Stan Ntwasa, a friend and close associate of Biko. I knew Stan, who was known as a radical black. That was something rare too. So, although this meant going to a 'white' party and having to play the game all over again I couldn't resist. It also meant free drinks. Steve was indeed there and, as fate would have it, it was Stan who asked me whether I would like to meet him.

So there I was, in front of this hovering black man, with an unbelievable presence. Steve shone in any gathering because of his deep interest in people, his sharp intellect and his eloquence. He was a gifted speaker and could spellbind any audience – black or white, intellectuals, working class or rural folk, young or old. I was immediately attracted to his intellectual handling of our main preoccupation, the evils of apartheid and the challenges to our community. But he could also talk about economics, literature, jazz or Marabi music. He was knowledgeable about African traditions and the history of our people. I was amazed at the range of his abilities.

I recall little about that first encounter. Steve was not particularly expansive and said nothing that was outstanding. It was only later that I got to know him better and he became a frequent visitor to my home.

Stan Ntwasa, who was working for the University Christian Movement (UCM) at the time, was my main link with the SASO group. But I quickly got to know and become friends with SASO's national organiser, Harry Rangwedzi Nengwekhulu, who was living in Johannesburg. Through him I learnt more about SASO and started writing articles about it. I was indeed privileged that the whole SASO leadership, particularly Steve Biko, took me into their confidence and began to frequent my house.

Steve became a regular visitor to my place whenever he came from Durban, where he was based, and our friendship was cemented. I also became good friends with Mamphela, who threw a small party at my home when she graduated from UNB as a doctor.

The SASO people drank a lot, argued a lot, womanised a lot and, apart from Barney Pityana, never went to church. Pityana later became a priest in the Anglican Church. I had given up my priestly studies in the Roman Catholic Church in 1964, because of its (then) silence over apartheid, and frankly I could not understand or agree with the teaching that we have to turn the other cheek; but I had not given up on God! Or should I say God had not given up on me! However, these were not ungodly people.

At various workshops held throughout the country, especially at the Wilgespruit Fellowship Centre in Roodepoort near Johannesburg, a frequently discussed topic was Black Theology and its place and role in our liberation struggle. One night, during one of these seminars, the security police raided us, ostensibly because we were staying in a white area without a permit. Among those arrested were Bishop Manas Buthelezi, Bishop Alpheus Zulu and Steve. We were all subsequently released with a warning to obtain permits – which we ignored.

Steve wrote extensively on religious issues. In his essay 'Black Consciousness and the Quest for a True Humanity' he claimed that it was the missionaries who confused the [black] people with their new religion. He wrote that it was when black people accepted Western religion that their cultural values declined.

> While I do not wish to question the basic truth at the heart of the Christian message, there is a strong case for a re-examination of Christianity ... More than anyone else the missionaries knew that not all they did was essential to the spread of the message. But the basic intention went much further than merely spreading the word. Their arrogance and their monopoly on truth, beauty and moral judgement taught them to despise native customs and traditions and to seek to infuse their own values into these societies.

He expressed his thoughts on Black Theology thus:

> Here we have the case for Black Theology ... let it suffice to say that it seeks to relate God and Christ once more to the black man and his daily problems. It wants to describe Christ as a fighting God, not a passive God who allows a lie to rest unchallenged. It grapples with

existential problems and does not claim to be a theology of absolutes. It seeks to bring back God to the black man and the truth and reality of his situation. This is an important aspect of Black Consciousness, for quite a large proportion of black people in South Africa are Christians still swimming in a mire of confusion – the aftermath of the missionary approach. It is the duty therefore of all black priests and ministers of religion to save Christianity by adopting Black Theology's approach and thereby once more uniting the black man with his God.

Had Steve lived longer than his 30 years he would certainly have become a national leader. How he would have lived his love life, one can only imagine. Steve's frankness about his love life might have led him to be seriously compromised in the jungle of politics and could have become a weakness in the area of moral issues that are facing our people today. Truthful he was, but wise perhaps he was not.

I was not sure whether I admired or envied his success with the ladies in those days; we were all caught up with the illusion of 'conquests'. I certainly realised later that this was a serious problem in the political life of our country ... and continent. The attitude towards women displayed by our leaders in business, in education, in politics, in the Church and in the domain of arts and culture is very problematic. The same can be said about the attitude towards the sanctity of the family. It was wanting in my friend Steve, and would have been an unfortunate message for the youth of today, faced with unexemplary behaviour from people in high places; some of whom aspire to high office.

Had Steve lived and run for office today he might never have made it. His vision of a new dispensation was so radically removed from anything we see today in the policies of the ruling party that he – like Azapo, the party that is still regarded as the torchbearer of his ideas – would never have had the ear of black voters. He would not have been part of the Greed and Grab Brigade – the 'I did not struggle to be poor' comrades.

Not that we should sanctify poverty. Far from it. We must create enough wealth for all. 'From each according to his abilities to each according to his needs' would seem appropriate here. Steve's motto would have been: 'We care for people!'

But on the political front, I wonder if he would have embraced socialism. Xolela Mangcu, one of Steve's most ardent and articulate followers and torchbearers, has written: 'Looking back on the days of my political activism, I realise I was never much of a socialist or a capitalist. I have always seen myself as a child of the middle classes of the Eastern Cape.' I believe there are many people who fit snugly into this category today. The ruling party is bogged down by this syndrome – its problem is the greed that has gripped its leading cadres. They talk socialism and act capitalism.

Steve would have had problems with that. He had his shortcomings, but greed for riches was not one of them. He loved to party, he loved the ladies. But he loved the people too. He certainly did not stay clear of them. Steve was close to the people, as can be deduced from his work. His commitment was totally to the liberation of the black people, especially the poor and degraded. But he was also committed to the middle classes, of whom he was one.

The projects he set up – the clinic at Zanempilo, the Black Community Programme (BCP), the Black Workers Project, the *Black Review* – an annual survey of contemporary events and trends in the black community, his involvement with the beginning of the Union of Black Journalists, his input into the creation of the Black People's Convention, and his role in creating the youth movement – the South African Students' Movement (led by Tsietsi Mashinini) as well as the Southern African Students' Movement (led by Onkgopotse Tiro); his support for the armed struggle (when we dared not even dream in that direction) and his commitment to political unity among the oppressed of South Africa and of Africa; all these attest to his allegiance and loyalty to his people and to his selflessness. Had he lived and become a leading Black Economic Empowerment (BEE) beneficiary, he would still have kept his roots where he belonged.

My work at the *Daily Mail* came to an abrupt end in June 1972, during SASO's General Students' Council (GSC) meeting in Hammanskraal north of Pretoria. This led to even closer collaboration with Steve, who was heading the Black Community Programmes with Bennie Khoapa in Durban. Steve had been expelled from UNB and had to abandon his dream of becoming a medical doctor. We all understood that it was his political commitment and his leadership of the BCM that cost him his place at the university.

I covered the GSC meeting in Hammanskraal where students referred to themselves as 'black'. This was the term I used in my copy. But the ever-vigilant sub-editors at the *Daily Mail* faithfully stuck to the paper's stylebook – and to the norms of white society – and changed 'black' to 'non-white'. This was the ultimate insult to the students as well as to me. To be non-white was to be defined in terms of others. It said the world was occupied by white people, and those who were not white were nothing.

The *Daily Mail* would have to change with the times. But I was not going to hang around and wait for them to do so. I resigned on the spot and Steve supported my decision. As I was a member of SASO's Johannesburg branch, the Reef Students' Organisation (Reefso) – at the insistence of Nengwekhulu, I had enrolled with Unisa – I went back to the conference as a delegate, to loud applause. My wife was aghast to learn that I was no longer employed. We had two children to feed! But she accepted it. Months later, the paper changed its policy and we became 'blacks'.

Steve suggested I come and work for one of the Black Consciousness projects, which I did. I was appointed Director of the BCP in Johannesburg, a post I held until I left for exile after a period of imprisonment for breaking my banning orders.

Steve Biko called himself the Son of Man – identifying himself with the greatest revolutionary of all time, Jesus of Nazareth. And, in a sense, he truly believed in the teachings of the Son of Man. One of his favourite verses was from Luke 4:18-19: 'He hath sent Me to heal the brokenhearted, to preach deliverance to the captives, and recovering of sight to the blind, to set at liberty them that are bruised ...' This became the centrepiece of the BCM's approach towards religion and politics and the guiding light for our activities.

Quoting from the SASO newsletter, and especially from Steve's column, 'Frank Talk', became a great source of inspiration for the followers of Steve Biko and the BCM in general. Now, more than 30 years later, some of the articles Steve wrote in those early days of the BCM I still find inspirational. And, what's more, I am finding even more in them than I did before.

What we were all about in the early 1970s and well into the 1990s was political and economic freedom – the freedom to govern or misgovern ourselves, as the Ghanaian leader Kwame Nkrumah once put it. Early on in our political thinking and development we began to consider the economic issues we would have to deal with. The in-thing was socialism and we became ardent socialists. But I never discerned any real enthusiasm from Steve for socialism; at least he never displayed it in public.

What led to a number of us taking the route into exile was a series of discussions, in some of which Steve participated. A number of students were growing tired of endless talk about fighting the 'system' without any real fighting taking place. We were frustrated by what we called the 'psychological and mental freedom' we aspired to achieve, and realised that unless we fought real battles for the control of the country we would be forever stuck at the level of raising fists in defiance of the apartheid monster, without making dents in its machinery.

We were being arrested and harassed daily, and raising our fists and shouting '*Power*' was getting us nowhere. We were desperate to move into some form of concrete programme. Anything would do. Yet nothing was planned.

I made up my mind to leave and to join the liberation movement, without really knowing where to find the armed struggle I was so determined to pursue. Steve thought it was too early to embark on such a programme. He was still hopeful of bringing about unity between the ANC and the PAC and he died in 1977 still trying to do that. We did not believe it would happen. So, a number of us left for Botswana, where we started a small community of refugees.

Within weeks we were in contact with the 'home base': Steve and other leaders of the BPC and student structures. We operated under cover of being students fleeing from apartheid. Within months we had a programme underway for training cadres in military and guerrilla warfare in Libya, Syria and Iraq. Uganda's Idi Amin provided material and financial support, as did Libya. But the funds and the programme were controlled by the PAC and we became pawns in some of their internal squabbles and divisions.

Our programme was also hampered by intra-party fighting and rivalry between the ANC and PAC and by our own naïveté and inexperience. Our programme died before it could even begin when, to spite us, the PAC gave the game away to the Botswana authorities!

In 1978 the Botswana government threw me out of the country – without declaring me a prohibited immigrant. The alternative was that I would be deported back to South Africa. Liberation politics were not as simple as we thought!

Scores of people from the BCM are still paying a heavy price for the decisions taken during that period of rash thinking. Many ANC leaders have never forgiven us for not coming cap in hand to them from the start and legitimising their claim to being the 'only authentic' movement fighting for the liberation of South Africa.

We are still on our own, except for those who took ANC party cards for their own survival. Steve was a master of survival, but I wonder what he would have done in today's South Africa.

The slogan 'Black man, you are on your own' is often ascribed equally to Barney Pityana and Steve Biko. In it lay the subtle message that, despite years of political activity, the ANC and PAC had been unable to instil in black people the realisation that their liberation was in their own hands and in their hands only, despite – or perhaps because of – the support that came from whites, in the country and elsewhere. The great PAC leader Mangaliso Robert Sobukwe called these people 'Abelungu aba sithandayo' (whites who loved us).

Biko's lambasting of liberal whites in South Africa had a lasting effect on the liberation struggle – to this day, liberals are regarded with suspicion. We are slowly admitting to some of the early wisdom of the Bikos and Sobukwes through the government's BEE policy, despite the fact that only the very best of the party stalwarts seem to benefit while the rest of the people struggle. Yet, the white people are still calling the shots on the economic front. And future struggles will be around filling the stomachs of all the citizens of our 'Beloved Country'.

So, the black-white problem does not want to leave us. It has only been complicated by the 'nouveaux riches', who are determined to climb on the shoulders of their fellow blacks. Now it is becoming a class struggle! The workers are forgotten in the scramble by the comrades.

Something is needed to curb the mad drive towards success at any cost. Could Black Consciousness be the antidote? I doubt it. We need a deeper remedy than that; not palliatives. Africa (and the world) needs a spiritual revolution: in politics, economics, culture and social relations. Maybe Steve was on his way towards discovering this, in spite of being an ardent proponent of BC.

His commitment to BC also did not exclude him from interacting meaningfully with whites, liberals and all in pursuit of his goal to liberate black people. His whole involvement was a 'quest for a true humanity' for all, as is suggested in his essay of the same title.

I first became aware of Steve's multi-faceted attitude to white people when we were driving out of Mafikeng one morning on our way to Johannesburg. As we left the town we stopped at a café. There we found a white student Steve recognised, and he was quite happy to offer her a lift to Johannesburg. I was furious, embarrassed and confused by this 'friendship' with *abelungu aba sithandayo* but Steve's political theory did not exclude personal friendships with people of other races and he was never apologetic about it.

I learnt something about Black Consciousness that day, and about the man who is regarded as its founding father. Even today opponents of Black Consciousness accuse it of being anti-white, and yet, like the PAC and the Unity Movement before it, it espoused non-racialism. It was all about the demise of apartheid and inclusion in the white man's world, which is what we have today in South Africa.

When people describe Steve and his contribution they usually refer only to his political ideas, but what I have come to find comfort in is his contribution in the spiritual domain. It is there for all to see in *I Write What*

I Like. But one has to read these with discernment to understand him.

Steve's discourse on spirituality covers a lot of ground. It deals firstly with the obvious shortcomings of the so-called Christian message espoused by the churches in South Africa during the dark days of apartheid. But it also delves into the thinking and beliefs of the black people prior to – and after – the arrival of the white people and the 'conquest' of ideas and culture through colonisation. He deals in subtle ways with what can be termed Universal Concepts of Divinity when he describes the 'self' in the quest for liberation.

In 'Black Consciousness and the Quest for a True Humanity' Steve claims that Black Consciousness is an 'attitude of mind' and a way of life. He calls it 'the most positive call to emanate from the black world for a long time'.

> Its essence is the realisation by the black man of the need to rally
> together with his brothers around the cause of their oppression – the
> blackness of their skin – and to operate as a group to rid themselves
> of the shackles that bind them to perpetual servitude. It is based on
> a self-examination which has ultimately led them to believe that by
> seeking to run away from themselves and emulate the white man,
> they are insulting the intelligence of whoever created them black.

He then goes on to state that the philosophy of BC therefore expresses group pride and the determination of blacks to rise and attain 'the envisaged self'.

I have come to understand the 'self' as the reflection of the Universal Spirit in human beings. It is the essence of the Spirit of God in us and it resides in our hearts. This is what makes us human beings. Whether Steve saw it in this light I can never be sure.

He goes on to write:

> Freedom is the ability to define oneself with one's possibilities held
> back not by the power of other people over one but only by one's
> relationship to God and to natural surroundings.

Thus did Steve set out his ideas on God, spirituality and freedom. I found much inspiration in the above passage years later and asked myself why I had never before seen, heard and understood the man's spirituality.

It has dawned on me just how rich a legacy Steve Biko has left us. His friend Stanley Ntwasa used to call Steve, Muntu Myeza, Mapetla Mohapi, Mthuli Shezi, and other martyrs who died for the struggle, 'saints'. Maybe he had a point!

'If only Steve was here,' we hear many people moan. But he is gone. His legacy, too, is being forgotten. Forgotten and trampled upon by his countrymen. But sometimes I catch myself sitting up and wondering whether we would have listened to him in this new South Africa. He may not have been a saint but to me he was a prophet who foresaw that unless black people stood up for their own rights – and responsibilities – nobody else would ever do it for them.

For real change a spiritual transformation is needed. This is what I believe Steve would have discovered had he lived. He would have been a ripe 60 in 2006 and would have grown much more in wisdom.

His research, and that of other like-minded patriots, was surely going to lead us back to our roots – our spiritual roots. Africa's Renaissance lies in discovering its spirituality.

This is where I believe my contact with Steve Biko has led me. He advanced my quest for a true humanity through the questions he raised, and the answers he provided.

I am writing this recognition of Steve Bantu Biko from Pune City in India, where I am on a pilgrimage to continue the discovery of myself. I am writing this tribute to a loving son of Africa with the vision of an Africa that will one day find its truth and shine in the world as the Pure Knowledge of the Universe, the gift that God bestowed on Africa.

Lala Ngoxolo Mfo ka Bawo! Uyilwile! Rest in peace, my brother. You have fought a good fight.

At the funeral: Samora, Biko's son, holds on to his bottle on his mother's lap.
Biko's funeral was attended by 20 000 mourners. King William's Town,
25 September 1977.

8. Mathatha Tsedu

He shaped the way I see the world

I never met Steve Bantu Biko. I tried to attend his burial in Ginsberg, King William's Town, but was turned back by police on my way there from Polokwane. However, I have been to his grave twice since then – once on the day of the unveiling of his tombstone, and again in 2002, the day after former Minister of Police Steve Tshwete was buried.

But Biko has always been part of my life, shaping the way I see and interpret the world, while trying hard to stay true to the values and virtues of being black in South Africa. Born in Louis Trichardt, now Makhado, an area in which, until the 1950s blacks owned freehold title to property, I had relatives who worked at a school for whites.

They looked after the white children, cooking for them and cleaning up after them. Over weekends and late in the day during the week, we would visit our relatives at the school. In reality, we were going for the food. The leftovers from the tables of the *kleinbaasies* were very delicious.

Even then, at age six or seven, it did not escape my notice that our school, run by Catholic missionary nuns, did not provide these delicacies of bread with peanut butter or jam. Nor did my curious mind fail to note that we lived out of town, while whites lived in town. In fact, 'town' meant where white people lived.

These observations did not amount to political consciousness, they were just some interesting realities floating about in my mind. When the National Party, under Prime Minister Hendrik Verwoerd, abolished freehold areas, our very own Masagani was demolished, along with the more famous areas of Sophiatown in Johannesburg and District Six in Cape Town, and we were expected to move into bleak, colourless two-roomed matchboxes in Tshikota.

My father refused to do this and shipped us all off to Nzhelele, a rural area in the bantustan of Venda. I did not realise then that he was making some kind of protest. All I knew was that we were moving out of our comfort zone. There would be no more tasty leftovers from the *koshuis* (boarding school) and, more importantly, in Nzhelele I had to herd goats in the snake infested bush. I hated everything about the move!

And worse still, in this rural setting, there was nothing to read – not a newspaper in sight, no magazines, no books. Our home had no reading matter at all, not even a bible. Information was scarce, no one in the village had radios. We lived in a virtual vacuum.

The only piece of reading material one could subscribe to and receive for free was the government's propaganda magazine, *Mvelaphanda* (Progress), produced in Pretoria by the Department of Information. It was similar to today's *Vukuzenzele* (Get up and do it yourself). I became one of *Mvelaphanda's* most dedicated readers. I believed every word in it and would even write letters to the editor commenting on developments in our area, where a little vegetable market had been built. *Mvelaphanda* was shaping my politics. I was becoming tribal, and knew all the white ministers whose pictures filled the pages of the magazine.

Now and then, when I went to town, the reality of our hopeless poverty would stare me in the face, but *Mvelaphanda* told me we, as Vhavenda, should not hanker after what whites had built for themselves. Instead, we should follow our leaders, such as Patrick Mphephu, who was to become the first 'president' of the so-called independent homeland of Venda, and build Venda ourselves, as whites had built their own homes, towns and cities.

It seemed to make sense, except that I could not see how or when this great transformation of poor little Venda was going to happen. Then, during the Christmas holidays, when the migrant workers came home from Johannesburg, they would talk about politics and how black people were being arrested in the cities for fighting for their rights. Nelson Mandela was among those mentioned.

I began to get access to more reading material and became aware of the ironically named Venda Independence Party, formed to reject 'independence' for Venda. The party was saying whites were wrong and the country should remain intact. I felt they were right and fell in with them. Indeed, I even voted for them.

I also read in newspapers about Helen Suzman, at the time the only representative in Parliament of the opposition Progressive Party (PP – the present-day Democratic Alliance), and her fights with the government. The PP believed in a qualified franchise.This meant that all South Africans should have the vote, no matter the colour of their skin. But to vote you either had to have matric or immovable property of some defined worth.

These two qualification would mean all whites could vote, as their schooling was compulsory and free up to matric. But even if they failed to achieve matric, virtually all whites had houses or farms or money that would ensure that they qualified to vote.

On the other hand very few blacks would qualify. But liberal newspapers such as the *Rand Daily Mail* made out the PP's policy to be the ultimate opposition to apartheid. What's more, I believed this, and admired Suzman so much that I once wrote to her asking to spend my school holidays as her guest, prepared to work in her garden if she so wished. She refused.

When the PP won six seats in the 1974 whites-only election, meaning that Suzman would be joined in Parliament by people such as Frederick van Zyl Slabbert, I used my last pocket money to send the victorious lady a telegram congratulating her and the party on the victory. I had bought into the liberal propaganda hook, line, sinker and all.

The turning point in my life came in 1972 when I was a standard eight high-school student. A friend of mine, Sam Phupheli, was studying at Turfloop university (also known as the University of the North) together with Onkgopotse Tiro, who was about to become a household name in Black Consciousness circles. During the now legendary black university boycotts he came home with a South African Students' Organisation (SASO) newsletter and *Turflux*, the Turfloop Students' Representative Council magazine.

The English in the two publications was heavy. But I struggled with it, sensing the new ideas contained in the pages. The message from SASO was clear: To start with, 'Black is beautiful'. We were made in the image of God so there was no need to use skin lighteners and stretch our hair to try and be white, or even to use 'white' names.

At the time many women and some men who could afford skin lightening creams were burning up their faces for two weeks and then returning to an even darker shade of black than before.

SASO declared that we were black, not in colour, but in attitude. The newsletter contained words and terms I had never encountered before: Black Consciousness (BC), oppression, struggle, communalism, imperialism, freedom, socialism and communism. What did it all mean? Tucked away in that rural corner of South Africa I struggled with these new ideas. But the more I understood, the more excited I became. In particular, BC said to me we were all black, all oppressed, and that we needed to come together and unite to achieve our freedom.

I loved the idea that not everyone who was oppressed was black, but that 'black' was a way of life and a mindset that not only saw oppression as wrong but, more importantly, united with the likeminded to fight it.

BC told me this was our country, Azania – the whole of it, not some rural outback called Venda. It said that the settlers who were oppressing us had arrived from Holland in 1652 as 95 men and 5 women. They decided, without asking the locals, to use the Cape as a refreshment station so that they could supply passing ships with fresh water and vegetables. They made a garden and in time the garden grew all the way to Musina in the north. We were now slaves in our own country, reduced to making the world more comfortable and habitable for whites.

The *koshuis* peanut butter and jam loomed large in my mind.

94

I searched for more reading, and felt the new message should be heard by many more people. I would write all these slogans on my shirts and walk around as some form of mobile billboard, broadcasting revolution. I stopped combing my hair as I now felt that combs were part of the oppressive machinery of settler domination and that the true authentic African look was corn rows, as I remembered my late mother's hair. I was a native with attitude and wanted everybody to see that and know why.

I had, in the past, given myself the name Godfrey, and was even beaten up by some black guy because he felt I was debasing his relative by taking his name. But at the time a European name was a symbol of being with it and I did not want Johannes or Andries but something classy, like Godfrey. Even schools wanted you to have what they called a Christian name. African names were seen as backward.

With Black Consciousness talking more and more to me I reverted to Mathatha with pride, and anyone who called me Godfrey got a full dose of BC and how we should stop giving ourselves and our children slave names.

I was becoming black and proud. By then I understood that the Suzman strategy would only take a few educated blacks and make them honorary whites, but would deny the rest of the black world the vote. BC and, through it, Steve, was telling me that the right to vote is a universal human right that we attain merely by being citizens – not rich or educated citizens, just citizens. It was fascinating stuff that unshackled my bonded mind.

As I was about to sit for matric in 1974 I attended my first political meeting, organised by the Black People's Convention at Maungani, outside Thoho-ya-Ndou. There I heard angry black poetry and the rhetoric of articulate blacks such as Nkwenkwe Nkomo, who ridiculed apartheid and said BC called for an anti-racist society.

I still remember vividly the words of Reverend Tshenuwani Farisani, president of the Black People's Convention (BPC) at the time, saying that goats and sheep sleep in the same kraal without the world falling apart or them killing each other. He said, 'you will also find small, big, green and not so green flies sharing the space with the animals. Who says people, with a higher intellect than all these flies and sheep cannot live together?'

I had walked about 10 km to attend the meeting and I did not even feel the distance on my walk back. I was on cloud nine. I was liberated that day. Everything made sense. The bantustans were a machination to divide and rule us, so it did not matter whether it was Gatsha (Chief Mangosuthu Buthelezi, chief minister of the KwaZulu 'homeland') who spoke the language of opposition to apartheid while working within the system, or Mphephu, who was just a stooge – they were all serving the white regime's agenda.

The way to genuine freedom was through operating outside the system and making it fail. I wondered where these guys had been all along when I was wasting my time with Mickey Mouse stuff such as homeland stooges and propaganda magazines. The call was to conscientise; to spread the message of the new gospel called Black Consciousness. For me that meant converting everybody I met to the BC way.

I had dreams of reaching thousands and in 1977 I had a brainwave: I would join the post office as a trainee technician and learn how to make a transmitter which could be used to broadcast our message. To do this I had to work with very raw boers who thought I was just another kaffir who had nothing else in the world to do but serve them.

It did not take long before I disabused them of that notion. One wanted me to call him *baas* and I asked him what *baas* meant. He looked keenly at me and said it meant he was my boss. 'What does boss mean? I am employed by the post office and I see it as the only boss I have, no one else. And you are not the post office but an employee like me,' I told him. He turned red.

The other black workers, my fellow trainees and especially the general workers, said I was mad and would be fired. I told them I would rather be fired than succumb to oppression like that. It was the Steve Biko doctrine of dying with dignity rather than living as a slave. The mental and psychological liberation that Steve said was a prerequisite for physical freedom was upon me.

My co-workers were right. I was fired soon enough, but I walked out of there with my head high – but without the transmitter. Even so I was not going to be Steve's angry black worker who curses in the toilet and then comes out to subject himself meekly to ridicule once more. Steve had written that even the way one dies could be a way to mobilise people. I read into that that the way I carried myself must at all times help liberate my people.

The news that Steve had been killed in detention found me in the middle of my 'transmitter-for-the-revolution' course. My leader, the man who had unshackled my mind, had been killed by the jailers of Mandela. I was angry. I remember sitting with a newspaper and reading everything about the circumstances. I read about Minister of Justice Jimmy Kruger's callous remarks about hunger strikes and Steve allegedly bashing his head against the wall and how this man's death left the minister cold.

I seethed with anger but also understood that the struggle must continue. Many of my fellow activists in Venda were being rounded up by Mphephu's regime. The only reason that I was not in jail was simply that I was not in Venda. We would give Steve a funeral that would show the boers that they had started a fire they couldn't extinguish. We would use his death, as he himself had said, to advance the struggle.

Organising transport to travel to Ginsberg and people to go was a huge task. I skipped all my transmitter classes on those days. The revolution was more important. I read much of what Steve had written – about fear, about pride, and about commitment.

The black man 'cursing in the loo' – the assertion that the oppressors can only go as far as the oppressed allow them to and that we effectively had nothing to lose but the chains that bound us to slavery were the only things that made sense to me.

Steve said we were our own liberators and because we were the ones who felt the pain of oppression we carried the sole responsibility to bring down the system that oppressed us. Whites, Steve said, did not need to join black organisations to help the struggle, they needed to mobilise whites, who were the people propping up the regime, to bring it down. This, Steve said, was not because BC was anti-white, it was simply pro-black. The sophistication of the arguments was mind blowing for me and the logic irresistible. I was the person Jimmy Cliff was singing about in his famous song, 'Who feels it knows it'.

Steve died before I could meet him but I felt that we knew each other. I certainly knew him. So I would be there at the funeral to raise my fist high and show Steve that we had not been cowed by what had been done to him. He was going to be proud of my fist in the air, solid, unwavering amongst the many thousands I knew instinctively would be there.

But it was not to be. On our way from Polokwane, after passing successfully through six roadblocks, we were turned back at Parys in the Free State. We had lied our way through the others, saying we were a football team or on the way to a family funeral in whatever the next town happened to be, but it did not wash with the Parys lot.

'If this bus moves another metre further, I will arrest you,' the cop said to the driver, who turned the bus back. We were devastated, but sang songs of defiance. '*Aluta Continua*', we shouted. We heard that in Johannesburg the buses were damaged by police even before they could leave.

Back at my transmitter project the boers had cottoned on to my activities and I was fired. The revolution was not going to be stopped by the regime, though. I went into journalism to propagate the message of the greatness of our people, the correctness of our struggle, and how victory was ours even if it took many years and many lives. I felt that as I was not one of the guerillas waging the armed physical struggle, mine was the battle of the mind, the psychological battle that needed to be won for freedom to make sense.

For me, the clouds had cleared at Maungani and had been gone ever since. They killed Steve and stopped him from making further fresh direct inputs. But Steve does not need to be here physically to continue to inspire at least me. He liberated me in his lifetime and I have stayed free since, drinking from his writings any time I need to. For me he continues to live in the message of the love of ourselves and our people.

So, what does Steve Bantu Biko mean to me? What does he represent 30 years on?

Firstly, Steve represents the highest form of clarity in thought and analysis of both the general political situation in the country and the psychological condition of black people in South Africa.

Secondly, he was an example of the highest form of commitment to the ideals of freedom.

Thirdly, Steve was a keen strategist and tactician who knew when to make alliances, even with whites, if the end result would advance BC. His friendship with Donald Woods, who was editor of the *Daily Dispatch*, gave him access to a medium that would otherwise have been closed to him.

The debacle during the 1972 conference in Hamanskraal where *Rand Daily Mail* reporter Patrick Laurence continued to refer to SASO as a body of non-white students instead of using the term black, which SASO preferred, was an example of his astute acumen. As the other leaders called for Laurence to be kicked out, Steve spoke against it and said the journalist should be allowed to correct his mistake.

This became a major story and what it did was popularise the issue of the definition of black. When Laurence repeated the affront, Steve knew he had lost the battle, but the debacle had become a major issue in media coverage about blacks and 'Bantu' or 'non-whites'. SASO was quite clear. We were, as black people, not negatives of others but positively black. The *Rand Daily Mail* eventually conceded and changed its terminology.

Fourthly, Steve's role in attacking the balkanisation of the country through bantustans and separate so-called Indian and coloured political schemes by insisting on a unified black approach fostered an anti-tribal understanding of our situation across the entire black spectrum in the face of a major state-sponsored propaganda campaign for separation, and was a major achievement.

South Africa is today reaping the rewards of that foresight, as tribalism does not characterise our politics as it does in many post-colonial situations.

Lastly, Steve helped create a movement that, though weakened today, persists in providing an alternative view of what freedom could still become to make a more positive impact on the lives of marginalised and downtrodden blacks. And so, from the grave, Steve continues to live and to lead. And for me personally, he remains an inspiration to be a better me each day.

*At the inquest: Biko's mother Alice (front left), his wife Ntsiki (front right)
and his sister Nomandile Mvovo (1977). Then Minister of Justice, Jimmy
Kruger, told Parliament that Biko's death: 'leaves me cold.'*

9. Zithulele Cindi

White carnations and the Black Power revolution: they tried us for our ideas

Steve Biko was 25 years old when it happened: the 1972 mass walkout of black students protesting against inferior education at black universities throughout the country – Fort Hare in the Eastern Cape, Turfloop in Pietersburg, University of Natal (Black Section) and Ngoye University in Natal, and the University of the Western Cape in Bellville,.

I do not believe that there is anything superstitious about the number 25 and all I can say is that a coincidence seemed to have connected the coup of 25 April 1974 in Portugal and us in the Black Consciousness Movement (BCM) on 25 September 1974.

The young soldiers in the Portuguese army were weary of the war in the colonies in Africa and were preaching the message of peace. They stuck white carnations into the barrels of their guns as a sign of protest and all of Portugal followed suit, culminating in the coup d'état of 25 April 1974 in which Antonio de Spinola toppled the rightwing government of Marcello Caetano. Could it be that the wave of 'flower children', with their messages of peace, had made an impact? Portugal even entered a 'peace song' in the Eurovision Song Contest at about that time. Many of the BCM activists were either banned or arrested at about the age of 25. I was detained on 25 October 1974 after being on the run for a month following the Viva Frelimo

Rallies organised by the BCM on 25 September to celebrate the victory and independence of the people of Mozambique. When we finally went on trial in 1975 a number of us were 25 years old.

For a very long time the powers-that-be had been planning to act against us as we had proved to be the proverbial thorn in their oppressive flesh with our writings and pronouncements. A regular feature of the 1970s was the rounding up of activists by the Special Branch of the South African Police. They even used the infamous and much hated pass laws at the time as a pretext to detain people because, in most instances, we would challenge them to produce warrants before they could either search or raid a place. They would then send the uniformed police, who were empowered to arrest any black person for failing to produce a *dompas*.

On arriving at the police station we would be handed over to the Special Branch who would have a field day mocking and interrogating activists. Thereafter they would take the person home or to his or her office where they collected everything – letters, journals, pictures, works of art, photos, press cuttings, party documents – and almost anything they did not understand which they had laid their hands on during these raids and detention sprees. In fact, they had a larger collection of Black Consciousness writings in their possession than the authors themselves collectively.

One of the greatest contributions made by the BCM to the revolutionary struggle in our country is a rich tapestry of cultural artefacts. The Special Branch built an enviable archive of Black Consciousness writings and they might have been conscientised had they bothered to read and understand the material they confiscated instead of looking at it as part of the 'total onslaught'.

Things came to a head in 1974 when we decided to mark the fact that the people of Mozambique, our immediate neighbours to the east, would be voting themselves into power and exercising self-determination. We styled our celebrations the 'Viva Frelimo Rallies'. Our plan was to send emissaries to Mozambique to invite Frelimo leaders to address the rallies, or at least the main one. The plans were to be kept under wraps – we would only announce them once our emissaries returned. But as things turned out the news leaked out even before the people who were supposed to go had left.

The agents of the system of oppression believed that if we sent people out we would bring them back in accompanied by 'trained terrorists'. This agitated them and they responded by banning the main rally – due to be held at Curries Fountain. The BCM leadership, including the late Muntu ka Myeza, quickly convened a meeting in Durban and resolved that the rallies would go ahead regardless of the ban. When that act of defiance was announced anybody associated with the BCM was rounded up.

The action began at about 2.30pm on 25 September 1974. I had been sent to Turfloop University in Polokwane and was detained there for a few hours, but managed to get out the next day thanks to some police error. I had to go 'underground' for a month, basically keeping our fraternal friends in Botswana and the international community up to date by giving them a blow-by-blow account of who had been taken in and so on. I became a fugitive. That is when I developed the habit of running the office 'off site', from my pocket so to speak – it is a habit that has become ingrained. Another habit, at the time, was not to sleep in the same house more than two nights in one week. So I was sleeping all over the township without even telling some of my hosts that I was on the run.

On 25 October, when I had been on the run for a month, the police caught up with me in Thembisa, a township in the Kempton Park area. I had spent the night at an aunt's place. The manner of my arrest and the circumstances that led to it were almost amusing in their banality – the good intentions of a cousin who wanted to serve me tea led to my missing the train and having to reconnect by taxi. After the cup of tea I went down the road to a taxi rank where I opened a newspaper and waited for a taxi. But, instead of the taxi, a white security policeman cruised by. And that was the end of my days on the run. I was the last to be taken in and I was interrogated for a month by the Special Branch, who were excited that they had the secretary general in their hands.

The 29 initial detainees were kept in solitary confinement, isolated from each other. I was in a place called De Wildt'. And wild it was – there I connected with nature in that I studied the habits of different types of spiders from the web-spinning type to those that burrowed in holes in the wall waiting for prey to pass.

An interesting element of my detention is that the fact that I was isolated from the other inmates raised curiosity on their part. It was not long before we struck up a relationship of convenience – they would smuggle to me any old piece of reading material/newspaper in return for bread or a carton of milk.

I was kept there for three months before we were taken to court and charged under the Terrorism Act. There were thirteen of us in all including Aubrey Mokoape, Saths Cooper, Kaborone Sedibe and Nkwenkwe Nkomo. The charge sheet stated that we had conspired to overthrow the state by violent means; that we were fomenting hatred between the population groups, in particular between blacks and whites; that we were causing resentment among people by constantly reminding them that they were being oppressed, exploited, and denied basic human rights. And more importantly, that we denigrated the Bantustan minions by calling them puppets, while maintaining that the true leaders were on Robben Island. That was the gist and thrust of the charges against us.

We went on trial at the beginning of 1975, our numbers reduced to 13. The state could not sustain the charges against two of us, so they were dropped. Eventually nine of us stood trial and two became state witnesses. I was accused No 9.

We were initially represented by Ishmael Ayob and Associates, but we parted ways with Mr Ayob after the first two appearances – from the start we had been uncomfortable with him. At our first meeting we had complained that we had been assaulted in detention and we wanted him to raise this before the magistrate. Ayob did not want to raise the matter and, to us, a crop of defiant activists who did not recognise the authority that held us, he appeared to be too subservient to the authorities.

Shun Chetty took over as instructing attorney, working with advocates David Soggot, Harry Pitman and Roy Allaway. The initial appearances were before Judge Fritz Stein and the trial proper was before Judge Gerhard Boshoff, a senior judge at the time. We challenged the state on all the charges they put to us. We asked for further particulars and, when these were not forthcoming, applied for the indictment to be quashed. The judge, however, believed there was a case to answer.

We concluded that our trial should not only be fought legally but also politically. In all despotic and oppressive regimes the rule of law goes out of the window – many people came to trial having been assaulted, although the police denied the assault. Ironically, things the police denied in the 1970s and 1980s they admitted after 1994 when they were applying for amnesty through the Truth and Reconciliation Commission.

Our trial was a trial of ideas. It was about conscientising people about our philosophy, the philosophy of black people. It was a trial about saying: 'I am oppressed. I'm not living and enjoying full rights of a human being. We must fight this.' We were charged for saying that. The state used a lot of lawyers, a lot of police and a few activists. We understood that people had been broken under interrogation and torture and, in fact, some of those activists who testified were later declared by the state to be hostile witnesses.

One of the charges was that we were preparing people to leave for military training. I was personally charged with sending one of our secretaries general, Sipho Buthelezi, into exile. They brought in a comrade who is now a bishop to testify that indeed we took Sipho to Botswana with a view to having him receive military training and come back and overthrow the state by violent means. In his evidence the bishop said we had driven through the night and arrived early in the morning, sleeping in the bush because the border gates were closed. Early the next day we had driven back. The Judge asked: 'So where did you leave him?'

The bishop: 'We left him in the bush.'

The Judge: 'Do you know if he left?'

The bishop: 'I don't know, he may have crossed.'

The state's case fell apart there and then – Buthelezi had left the country on his own.

One major state witness was a man by the name of Harry Singh – he had been paid to send us to prison. After testifying he had no option but to join the police. He had sold out and life was unbearable for him. He died of frustration and melancholy.

The state relied largely on a book by an American author, entitled *Why Men Rebel*, using it to formulate their indictment. They called a political science lecturer, Professor Van Wyk, as their star witness. In response, we brought the author of the book, Ted Gurr, from the USA and put him on the box.

The state used a great deal of literature, in fact, all our writings on various topics. I was tortured because of my letters, all of which began with the salutation 'Dear comrade'. I was among the first to use this salutation because in the BC then the popular form was 'Brother'. I was taken to task about referring to others as comrades – to the state comrade meant communist – in those days, anyone who opposed the state was labelled a communist.

We called Steve Biko to explain that telling people they are oppressed is not necessarily an instruction to them to rise up against the state; that conscientisation is a necessary step in informing people about their circumstances. People were oppressed and denied basic human rights and the right to vote simply because they were black. This should not be, it was immoral. Blackness then was a state of mind, a philosophy.

When Steve agreed to testify on our behalf our lawyers had to apply for him to be released from his banning order and given indemnity. Our meetings with him gave us an opportunity to touch base with him. For most of us this was the first time we had seen him since his banning. In a way, we managed to hold a mini National Council meeting in the course of the trial.

Although Steve admitted during his evidence that it was he, not Strini Moodley (Accused No 8), who was responsible for the articles under the byline Frank Talk, he was not charged. With hindsight, perhaps if he had been charged, and been one of us, he would have been alive today.

Losing Steve was really devastating. When we parted ways at the Pretoria Supreme Court he was beginning to challenge a space within me that once belonged to Mthuli ka Shezi, my old contemporary from primary school who, when he was killed by the Boers, had driven me to vow that for his sake I could not give up, I had to continue fighting. No matter what!

In December 1976 we were convicted of conspiracy to overthrow the state by violent means; of having engaged in terrorist activities; of having fomented hatred of black people towards whites and of denigrating Bantustan leaders by calling them puppets.

We received various terms of imprisonment – I was one of those sentenced to five years for conspiracy.

Chained to one another, we were driven the same evening non-stop from Pretoria to Cape Town – a harrowing and terrifying drive. I was chained to the man who would one day become Minister of Defence, Mosioua Lekota.

On Robben Island our ideas were again tested. Because we were considered militant we were isolated and dubbed 'klip-gooiers' (stone-throwers), possibly because the hallmark of the 16 June uprisings was the stone. At the time of our arrival more than a thousand inmates were arriving at the Island – an avalanche of prisoners resulting from the uprisings.

We were put in the dormitory cells among a large number of young activists, who were all angry. We realised these young people were not politicised or conscientised. Some of them came from grassroots and had no training at all. Some were illiterate. So, using the experience we had gleaned from our work in the BC's community development programmes and literacy projects, we ran seminars and held political discussions. We told them that although we were behind bars we must not internalise prison, we must change the prison walls. We counselled those who were traumatised.

In our first two months on the Island we embarked on a hunger strike in protest against the poor food, the conditions under which we were being held, and the hard labour. On the fourth day of the strike, the authorities conceded. Hard labour was stopped and the quality of the food improved.

The prison authorities did not take kindly to that. We were seen as 'poisoning' the prisoners. The authorities, who believed that when people were imprisoned they would be cowed into submission, were surprised to find people continuing with defiance, upholding their dignity. So they came and weeded us out.

We were taken to 'A Section' where people such as Nelson Mandela, the late Walter Sisulu, Govan Mbeki, Wilton Mkwayi and others were kept. I was the youngest in that section at the time but we interacted well – I would remind them that, young as I was, I was the leader of my political movement – the youngest secretary general of a political group in the country at the time.

In 1977, when Kaiser Matanzima, Chief Minister of Transkei, was working hard to get the Xhosa-speaking political prisoners released so they could serve in the Transkei administration, I had no doubt that, as a Xhosa-speaker himself, Steve would have supported our challenge to those prisoners who so wanted to take up Matanzima's offer. We used every argument to discourage them from joining the Bantustan system, but they would not listen. We reminded these Robben Island prisoners that we had been sentenced, among other things, for eulogising them as the leaders of the people. When that failed to convince them, we issued an ultimatum telling them we would publicly dissociate ourselves from them. That convinced them. Steve belonged to such battles.

Thirty years later, I still feel the numbing pain that gripped us on the Island when we heard that Steve Biko had been killed in detention. It is not for me to speculate about what Biko would have done had he been alive today. To me he remains a mentor, a father and philosopher and all those things that help to shape a person into a complete human being. He is the lodestar that showed me the way in a quest for a true humanity.

At the inquest: Winifred Kgware holds up a photograph of Biko encircled by a wreath (December 1977). In a terse summing-up statement, the magistrate cleared any policemen of being responsible for Biko's death.

Courtesy of Drum Social Histories/Bailey's African History Archive/africanpictures.net

IO. Saths Cooper and Pandelani Nefolovhodwe

Steve Biko and the SASO/BPC trial

Steve Biko was a key defence witness in the South African Students' Organisation (SASO)/Black People's Convention (BPC) trial which ran from 31 January 1975 to 21 December 1976.

There were nine of us on trial: Saths Cooper, Muntu Myeza, Mosioua 'Terror' Lekota, Nchaupe Aubrey Mokoape, Pandelani Nefolovhodwe, Nkwenkwe Nkomo, Kaborone 'KK' Sedibe, Zithulele Cindi and Strini Moodley.

Steve would have been the first witness if he had been in Pretoria when the defence case opened in April 1976 but this lover of life itself, who felt severely confined in King William's Town's Ginsberg township, where he was banned and house arrested, chose to drive rather than fly the hundreds of kilometres to Pretoria.

The long drive gave him a degree of freedom to deviate along the way and travel through many magisterial districts between King William's Town and Pretoria, which he would otherwise not have been able to do. Typically, he chose to defy the terms of his banning order and not to apply for permission from the chief magistrate of King William's Town before leaving. He relied on the knowledge that the police dared not prevent him from appearing before Judge Boshoff at the 'Palace of Justice'.[1]

So it was that Rick Turner, a political science lecturer at the University of Natal, became the first defence witness in the historic trial.[2] He had a torrid time. Saths Cooper, the first accused, was in the witness stand for about a week, and then Steve took the stand.

The assistant prosecutor, Kevin Attwell, had the unfortunate task of cross-examination and, time after time, proved to be no match for Steve's formidable intellect. John Rees, the Deputy Attorney-General, who was chief prosecutor, either underestimated Steve's importance or anticipated that in the cut and thrust in court Steve would not emerge intact.

Count One on the charge sheet alleged that the accused:

> during the period of 1st July 1971 to September 1974 at a place or places to the prosecutor unknown acting through and/or in the name of SASO and/or BPC, wrongly, unlawfully and with intent to endanger the maintenance of law and order in the Republic or any portion thereof conspired each with all the others, to commit the following acts to wit:
>
> a   acts to bring about a revolutionary change of the political, social and economic system of the Republic, by unconstitutional and/or violent means or by the threat of such means, and/or
>
> b   acts to cause, encourage, or further feelings of hostility between the white and other   inhabitants of the Republic.

It became very clear that it was the philosophy and ideology of Black Consciousness that were on trial. From the onset we decided that our defence was that there was nothing wrong with our activities or those of SASO and the BPC. This line of defence was pursued by every witness who testified on our behalf. Steve Biko went even further, indicating that he should have been in the dock with the accused.

Steve's exchanges with the prosecutor are legendary now. Who can forget Denzel Washington's portrayal in the movie *Cry Freedom*, where it was put to Steve that his skin colour was not 'black'? Steve's famous retort that the prosecutor similarly was not literally 'white' had the packed courtroom in stitches. The exchanges were an education, almost those of a teacher barely tolerating his recalcitrant pupil, who absolutely refused to understand simple concepts.

Steve took full advantage of his short testimony to expand on his writings; particularly the critical import of being black in a race-obsessed society and the actual meaning of Black Consciousness. There was a stir when Steve referred to certain of his *I Write What I Like* articles, which had been wrongly ascribed to Strini Moodley, who edited the SASO newsletter. Nevertheless, Strini remained charged with writing articles that he did not write and was convicted of 'common cause' conspiracy. A standing joke during detention without trial was that security police desperately sought the whereabouts of one 'Frank Talk', who penned the *I Write What I Like* articles, not believing that it was a pseudonym, and often demanding to know from many of us during detention *'Waar is Frank?'* (Where is Frank?) Imagine the disbelief when Strini claimed that he was Frank; but the protectors of white supremacy got their vengeance on both Strini and Steve!

The apartheid state had framed its case against those who were at the forefront of organising the 'Viva Frelimo Rallies' to celebrate Mozambique and Angola's independence after the fall of the Portuguese military regime. But agents of the state quickly realised that if they had given the matter more thought they could also have charged Steve and a few other leading BC supporters. The 'Viva Frelimo Rallies' were seen as activities which furthered the notorious doctrine of common purpose among the accused, SASO and the BPC to overthrow the apartheid state.

During the period 25 September 1974 (when the rallies were scheduled) and 31 January 1975 (when the first of numerous court appearances in the trial took place) well over 300 activists were arrested in various parts of the country and held under the infamous Section 6 of the Terrorism Act. This feared legislation allowed for indefinite detention in solitary confinement without trial. Steve was not among those arrested and none of us ever implicated him as the luminary of the BC ideology; we acknowledged our own roles and assumed responsibility for actions that were not ours personally. Thus it was that Strini Moodley did not deny that he was responsible for the *I Write*

What I Like articles and paid for it with seven years of imprisonment.

Steve was somewhat disappointed that his stint in court was short-lived – his cross-examination was shorter than his evidence in chief, ending on the second day. He believed that his long drive to Pretoria would have been more justified if he had had the opportunity to remain there for a few more days. At the end of his testimony he was permitted to join us in the holding cell at the court premises. In this last meeting we discussed many factors confronting the movement, including continuing with the unity talks with other liberation movements. We also touched on the necessity of linking up with BC cadres who were in exile to make sure that the activities of the movement continued.

Steve was a tremendous asset to our largely white defence team, who began to understand Black Consciousness in its context in South Africa. He painstakingly went through all the statements we had made while we were in detention, providing various insights for the defence team. His parting with the accused was quite poignant – he told us not to expect to be discharged. The next time he came to Pretoria (18 months later) it was against his will and it was there that he died a terrible death.

When then Cape Town attorney Abdullah Omar, who would become Minister of Justice in 1994, got permission to visit Robben Island soon after Steve's death in detention and conveyed the terrible news to Terror' Lekota it was a defining moment for all of us. Each of the nine of us who were incarcerated in the isolation cells in Robben Island's 'C Section' were in shock.

The question is often asked, especially during stormy tendentious debates between competing political entities, 'If Steve Biko were alive, where would he be?' There have also been the inevitable eulogies, particularly from neophytes and those who uncritically cling to specific parts of Steve's writings. It is clear that if Steve were alive we would be in a qualitatively different country – more compassionate, more cherishing, less self-engrossed, less self-destructive.

Steve Biko was a man among men, a leader among leaders, quick to acknowledge fault, easy to engage with, but a foe to be reckoned with (which probably resulted in his death). His was not a mindless quest for personal aggrandisement or ego-tripping. He revelled in contentious intellectual engagement, was never churlish, never mean; always encouraging, ever recognising of potential; comfortable with himself, never feeling threatened. All of these were the qualities that he lived by and amply demonstrated during his milestone testimony in the SASO/BPC Trial.

---

1   In the mid-eighties the same Judge Boshoff heard the application by Drs Joe Veriawa, Dumisani Mzimane, Tim Wilson and Professors Frances Ames, Phillip Tobias and Trefor Jenkins to force the SA Medical & Dental Council to try the medical practitioners who were guilty of gross negligence and ethical violations in relation to the death in custody of Steve Biko. Judge Boshoff feigned ignorance of Biko, but granted the application!
2   Turner was assassinated by the Security Police in his home in Durban in 1978.

Biko's wife Ntsiki, his mother Alice and his brother Khaya at a press conference after the inquest.

Courtesy of Selwyn Tait, *Sunday Times*, Johnnic Communications.

II.

Duncan Innes

A white man remembers

Steve Biko's contribution to the liberation struggle in South Africa is well known, even if it may not always have been fully acknowledged. But I owe him a debt of gratitude for the major contribution he made to my personal intellectual and political development.

I first met Steve in mid-1967 at a congress of the National Union of South African Students (NUSAS). Steve was a member of the University of Natal delegation and I was a young member of the University of Cape Town delegation. Born and bred as a middle class, white South African, I had already developed some rather vague liberal ideas as well as a strong mistrust of apartheid, especially after I was forced to endure nine long months of compulsory military service. But at that time my opposition to apartheid was more emotional than intellectual and my understanding of black oppression was at best naive.

Then I met Steve.

The 1967 NUSAS congress, which was held at Rhodes University, was torn apart from the start by the University's decision that African students could not stay in residence on campus during the congress along with their white counterparts. Instead, they had to stay in the township. NUSAS passed a resolution protesting against the University's racism, but for Steve this was not good enough. He made a fiery speech in which he argued that the predominantly white NUSAS leadership needed to take a stronger stand against the University's position – a stand in which they showed their willingness to suffer along with their black counterparts. He proposed that we all embark upon a 24 hour hunger strike.

I was completely blown away by his speech. To start with I had never before heard a black person speak so eloquently and powerfully about the way in which apartheid sought to degrade black people. And, secondly, I had never before been asked to make a personal sacrifice, even for only 24 hours, in support of my anti-apartheid beliefs. I spoke in support of Steve's motion and, along with the majority of the congress, voted for his hunger strike.

During the remainder of that congress I got to know Steve quite well. The first thing that struck me was that he was willing to spend time outside of formal congress sessions with me, a young white student, to help me understand how black people experienced apartheid. This lesson was invaluable in helping me to understand black oppression, not only socially and politically, but also psychologically and intellectually. I also learned from him that the struggle against apartheid was one in which there was no middle ground: you were either part of the problem or part of the solution. But, surprisingly to me, I also discovered something else about Steve during that week, which was that his strong commitment to opposing apartheid did not rule out a readiness to enjoy life to the full, including a healthy capacity to party. We had some good times that week.

Later that year I was elected President of the UCT SRC and, in that capacity, met with Steve and black student colleagues of his on a number of occasions. I was by then an activist student leader, heading inexorably towards a confrontation with the apartheid government and, as such, I drew hungrily on the debates and radical ideas of black student leaders to help guide my own political decisions. At this time Steve and his close colleagues, such as Barney Pityana, were openly advocating their ideas on Black Consciousness and it was fascinating for me to be party to these debates. But my participation also brought with it a growing sense of unease. As Steve began to articulate the view that whites could not be part of the solution in South Africa because they could not experience what it meant to be black under apartheid, I began to wonder what role whites like myself could play in the struggle. Did we, in fact, have a role?

Despite these concerns, there was no questioning the personal commitments that Steve had towards his white friends and student colleagues. In fact, I was sufficiently close to Steve that, at the next NUSAS congress at Wits in 1968, he was one of two student leaders to nominate me for NUSAS President. I have no doubt that his public support was a key factor in my being unanimously elected President.

Throughout my term as NUSAS President, Steve and I kept in contact. When he came to Cape Town, where I was based, he would stay with me and we would party until late at night, with Steve hurriedly using the back exit when the police came banging on the front door, returning after they had gone. And on my frequent visits to Durban, where I met with black and white students who were part of the NUSAS community there, I would always spend time with him, Barney and others to discuss the role that black and white students could play in challenging apartheid.

By then it was clear that the South African Students Organisation (SASO), which Steve and others had formed, would at some stage pull the black student campuses out of NUSAS to which many of them were then affiliated. While I understood this, I was concerned about the impact which the withdrawal of black students would have on NUSAS. As NUSAS President, my objective was to try and position the organisation as part of the struggle against apartheid and I worried that NUSAS would become more conservative without the black students who were its key radical wing. On the other hand, Steve's primary objective was for SASO to provide an organisational base for the mobilisation of black students in the anti-apartheid struggle - and white students in NUSAS were largely irrelevant to that endeavour and may even be perceived to impede it. While Steve and his colleagues always welcomed the support they received from white students, they were adamant that a truly non-racial student movement was not possible at that stage of the struggle against apartheid.

However, despite these strategic differences, the leaderships of both SASO and NUSAS maintained good relationships with one another – and Steve was key in ensuring this. So when SASO finally split from NUSAS after I had left due to ill- health, the two organisations operated as separate student wings in the common struggle against apartheid. I have no doubt that the experiences which Steve and many other black and white student leaders, including myself, had shared together earlier contributed to the amicable way in which the split occurred.

In 1972 I left South Africa to continue my post-graduate studies in England and lost touch with Steve. Five years later, while I was still in England – in September 1977 – I heard that Steve had been brutally murdered by the forces of apartheid. A wave of sadness overwhelmed me that terrible day, partly because I knew that South Africa had just lost one of its greatest sons and future leaders, but also because I knew that the man who had changed my life was gone.

Biko's son Nkosinathi listens attentively to proceedings at the Truth and Reconciliation Commission hearings (East London, 1997). Five former security policemen admitted to being involved in Biko's death and applied for amnesty.

Courtesy of Benny Gool/Oryx Media Productions/africanpictures.net

I2. Jonathan Jansen

King James, Princess Alice, and the ironed hair: a tribute to Stephen Bantu Biko

From afar

The times were angry. Things were going from bad to worse at home during the middle to late 1980s. We were mobilising against the regime on both sides of the Atlantic. And I was delighted to see how students on American campuses were responding to the disinvestment campaign, forcing universities in that country to withdraw their financial holdings in companies doing business in apartheid South Africa.

Despite our political work as South African students on foreign campuses there was the guilt of distance, the feeling of not being able to be with my high school students as stories of torture, killings, detentions and disappearances kept coming through to my place of study and activism in California.

I had recently returned from a large conference of angry black South Africans in Tennessee, in the south of the United States, where I was elected secretary of the Student Representative Council leading this group of students studying in the USA. There, the ANC representative at the United Nations, the brilliant medical student David Ndaba (his exile name), lifted our spirits with his closing remarks: 'Let's march, right now, to

Pretoria.' There, G M Nkondo fortified our commitment with his thunderous admonition: 'black man, you are on your own!'. With those words, of course, the need for another Steve Biko surfaced in all night discussion among all of us, including some of those comrades loyal to congress politics. The times were very angry.

At about this time Richard Attenborough released his film *Cry Freedom*, and a whole contingent of South African comrades and anti-apartheid American activists descended on a cinema in San Francisco to watch the movie on opening night. For the South Africans it was a rare but powerful opportunity to make a connection, any connection, to what was happening back at home; it did not matter that this was a Hollywood depiction of a distant struggle. The theatre was packed to capacity, mainly with black people, all activists. It was the first time I had sat in a movie and felt an audience constantly speaking back at the criminals masquerading as police; but for the most part, the audience was relaxed. And then it happened. As Steve Biko was being interrogated and tortured in the movie, he leapt out of his chair and swung a few almighty blows, hitting the policemen in attendance. As if under choreographic instruction the entire movie audience jumped to its feet and applauded loudly. What a release!

As a child

As the 30th anniversary of the death of Steve Biko, great thinker and strategist, approaches I remember how he changed my life as a teenager desperate to find a language and identity through which I could understand the terrible experience of dispossession and humiliation of those apartheid years. I hated everything about whiteness; what it did to my parents as they shrank in front of suburban madams and what it did to my neighbours, people forcibly removed from their integrated neighbourhoods, now declared 'white'. Most of all, I despised what other people called me: 'Coloured'.

It is impossible to understand the power of Biko's message and his movement without some insight into what it was like growing up as a teenager in conservative Cape Town during the early 1970s. My parents worked for white people. My father brought home stories of the white madams in Rondebosch and Lansdowne, of their tantrums and tempers. He named his youngest son after madam's son. My mother was dressed in perfect whites as a nurse at a hospital that basked in its English colonial name: Princess Alice Orthopaedic Hospital, where she often took orders from white doctors and white matrons alike. My mother had an assertive streak in her that, at full blast, respected neither colour nor status; but this was kept within bounds so as not to lose her nursing job that kept the family above the poverty line.

But it was in church that I felt the full venom of white consciousness. I belonged to a curious assembly, a church established in the Cape by English, Scottish and Irish missionaries. The Brethren, as they are still called, epitomised English culture and custom in everything they did. The sisters wore modest English dress to church, with hats covering all their hair, long dresses, stockings and sensible shoes. The brethren wore ties and jackets and perfect haircuts. The only bible tolerated was the King James version. The prayers and hymns were laced with old English expressions such as 'thy' and 'thee'. Many a newcomer to this church would find him or herself severely reprimanded for trying to speak in the natural language of the township; after some time stammering through this foreign English, the native would be tamed and socialised into the fold. Perhaps Biko had a point when he talked about the transformations of Christianity over time, yet noted that 'somehow when it landed in the Cape, it was made to look fairly rigid'.

The church conferences were a display of white European racial and cultural dominance. The main speakers (Anderson, Moore, Brandon, McGrath, McConnell, Tatford) did the teaching and preaching, and the natives listened in endless admiration. In time the native brethren rose to prominence and would 'share the platform' with these European stars; and they mimicked their patrons perfectly, even in name (Dudley, Jardine, De Vries). Yet for all this piety and pretence the white brethren fed lavishly off the fruits of apartheid, ensuring that even within church gatherings there was a clear segregation in seating arrangements – whites in front in designated seats, blacks at the back in their own seats.

Even more bizarre was the way the so-called 'fellowship' was racially ordered. My most striking memory was the annual 'conference' of churchgoers in the Maitland Civic Centre. There, after an intense ministry to the saints, lunch would arrive and, as a teenager, I noticed that the blacks either went out to their cars or onto the lawn, or stayed seated in the hall. We would then produce our tins of food and flasks of tea and eat the humble sandwich, not a white saint in sight. So one day I decided to follow the whites and noticed that they all disappeared through a side door. I slipped past the crowd and opened the side door. There, to my utter amazement, sat all the white saints around a large table sagging with the most impressive roast meats, fruits and desserts, served, of course, by some of the natives. After the interval black and white saints reconvened in the centre hall as if nothing had happened.

I often think that my attraction to Black Consciousness started the day I opened that door.

Ironed hair

Nowhere was the script for Black Consciousness more clearly written than in that community of South Africans loosely called 'coloureds'. A continuing preoccupation of white racism and paternalism in equal measure, the coloureds were created through a mix of laws and policies that seduced them with the promise of elevated social status, a better income and guaranteed labour preferences that would separate them from those at the lowest end of the racial spectrum – the Africans in Langa, Gugulethu and Nyanga. Often darker skinned, the Africans now became less desirable than the whites, and skin colour became then and continues now to be a firm marker of status, together, of course, with that other curiosity, hair.

Hair – it is the kind of subject that still gives entertainer Marc Lottering 80 per cent of his comedic material. This is hard to understand unless you can imagine your aunt bent over a hot machine wrapped in paper and having her hair straightened at some risk so that she can turn this otherwise beautiful adornment, well, white. I can still smell the aroma of burnt hair. She called her head adornment 'naughty hair', something I would only understand many years later after reading literatures about the colonisation of the mind.

Hair was a sore point in this world of white consciousness. An uncle who had too many children still tells the story of how he would be called at work to say he had a beautiful daughter or son, and he knew that it was simply because the kid was fair with straight hair. The more terse announcement – 'Maggie had another child' – spelt gloom, darkness and curly hair. But of course hair futures were not that easily determined at birth for a child just emerged from a narrow canal covered in straightening fluids over a largely bald patch. But there was always an aunt ready to set the record straight: *'Daai hare sal nog krul!'* (that hair will go frizzy yet'). In other words, do not get your hopes up.

It was hair and skin that caused my late father-in-law to boot me and his daughter out of his house with two hours' notice when we did the traditional thing: 'asking to go out' – to court his daughter. Until that moment I had figured he liked me since he would call me to preach in his church and expressed support for my youthful faith. Liked, that is, until his daughter and I requested his blessing, not for marriage, but simply to enjoy 'going out' together. The pressure was on him and his family from the saints; an elderly sister in the church told his daughter to be concerned about 'what the children will look like'.

This is the world into which I was born, where the pain of racial abuse came equally from white hands and from black. It was everywhere in this coloured township. From the local 'bubby', the Indian shopkeeper, who stared at me as a six-year-old and shouted for all to hear: 'Come listen, this kaffir speaks English!' to the long trip in a railway bus to the town of my birth, Montagu, having to witness black people sitting on top of each other at the back, while only one or two persons occupied the white section in the air-conditioned front of the bus. I recall a youthful anger as I struck out verbally at the white bus driver on arrival in Montagu, angry that my dignified mother had to be squashed for hours at the back of this half-full bus.

Higher things

One thing was clear even then – my active church life had no answers to this brutality. While I appreciated the fellowship of black saints, the service of the Gospel, the life of faith, and a believing family whose spiritual commitment shielded me from the vices and violence of the Cape Flats, there was no solution offered for dealing with racism in and outside the church. Quite the opposite – in this community of saints the scriptures were clear: 'Our citizenship is in heaven'. This is probably not what the apostle Paul meant, but it was a handy rebuff every time I inquired about the tyres burning in the streets outside while we sang inside about God's 'Amazing Grace'.

Years later I would find Biko speaking about 'the appalling irrelevance of the interpretation given to Scriptures' and his astute observation that 'the Church further adds to [black] insecurity by its inward-directed definition of sin and its encouragement of the *mea culpa* attitude'.

Scraping through high school, and unable to enter the university closer to my home (a race permit and a good pass was required), I shuffled off to the University of the Western Cape (UWC), a university reserved for coloureds in Bellville on the other side of Cape Town – three hours' travel back and forth using four modes of transport. It was a daily journey I hated intensely: constantly tired, academically under-prepared, not enough money to make the journey every day, and a racist club of Afrikaner academics who kept reminding students about the limits of their ability.

And then a friend dragged me along to 'the café' at UWC and there, on a table, stood a man who represented in charisma and content the image of Steve Biko. I was never so entranced in my life as when Allan Boesak, mainly in Afrikaans, spoke to the growing anger and resentment that I felt as a black person. Until then nobody had called us black: 'coloured' was what I heard all the time. This young, handsome, articulate man with the stylish 'afro' spoke directly to my needs; he gave me a language with which to make sense of my experiences and, to one who sang unthinkingly about being 'whiter than snow' in the gospel chorus, here was a Christian whose message was influenced by another kind of Christianity – Black Theology. Most importantly, his embrace of black identity made no reference to coloureds/Indians/Africans – we were all oppressed, in various ways, and everything else was divisive of black community. He quoted liberally from Biko in the Eastern Cape, from black theologians in the USA, and from liberation theologians in Latin America.

It would not be sacrilegious, I hope, to borrow from another gospel song: 'It was there by faith I received my [political] sight'.

Writing b(l)ack

Biko's assertion of blackness not only as an oppressed identity but also as an assertive one explained the mushrooming of afros among my black friends and the instant attacks on any unsuspecting township dweller who dared to refer to him or herself as 'coloured' or 'Indian' or 'Xhosa'. In one move, black identity became not only a means of organising oppressed groups on the basis of a common experience but a way of chipping away at the certainties that apartheid assigned to ethnic labels.

It is Biko's call for assertiveness of the black condition that made such a major difference to the lives of many South Africans. It forced another look at the fragility of whiteness, its false power, its presentation of itself as a single model of goodness. To be black, now, was to say so; it was to wear black and speak back; it was to elevate black culture, traditions and practices from their denigration (note the exchange with Judge Boshoff on the meaning of witchcraft in Biko's trial) as something beautiful, intriguing and blessed.

But it was in writing back that Biko had his greatest influence on the lives of many, including me; turning the tables on the relationship between knowledge and authority so that we ceased to be consumers of official history written by white authorities of all ideological leanings.

I understood this to mean, in my own work, that black people should step away from their awe of white writings and lead scholarly writing about things they knew well but never dared to commit to paper because of a sheer lack of confidence. The importance of this shift within black academic and scholarly work from knowledge-consumer to knowledge-maker cannot be overstated. It is a psychological, emotional and political shift that is as liberating to black scholars as it is intimidating to many white scholars.

This was the kind of political attitude that led to the production of my first book, *Knowledge and Power in South Africa*, published in 1991 by Skotaville Press. It was only in part an attempt to show how the social and natural science disciplines were implicated in the apartheid project; the disciplines were not merely conveyors of apartheid ideology, they created and sustained the myths of white supremacy and black subordination. It was, however, also an attempt to demonstrate what happens when black academics take the lead in writing about subjects that few besides Archie Mafeje, Es'kia Mphahlele and Chabani Manganyi had redefined intellectually. What was crucial about the assembly of authors in *Knowledge and Power* was that while black editors and authors led the writing in major disciplines they did so with the participation of progressive white scholars in a secondary but collaborative role. In tone and substance, therefore, the book owes its emergence to the powerful role of Steve Biko in my life as a graduate student and a new scholar.

There is trouble ahead, though, for all major signposts point to a coming crisis in black research leadership and productivity. The familiar narrative of ageing white males still dominating the research corpus with no clear signs of their replacement is not an exaggeration. Despite millions of rands being invested every year in capacity-building initiatives there is little to show in terms of a visible new generation of black academics and researchers. The implications are profound, for it means the replacement generation, especially in competitive disciplines like genetics and mathematics, is likely (again) to consist of young white scholars trained in the best laboratories in the country.

The problem here is only partly one of access and opportunity. It is still largely a problem of personal confidence, of intellectual assertion, and of occupying the ample space provided in this open society. I have trained and graduated enough doctoral students in the past 15 years to recognise the enduring problem of black reticence and withdrawal in the face of academic power. It expresses itself in writing in the third person, in concealing personal voice, in dismissing the authority of experience, and in hiding behind the power of external authority (the famous professor) in an almost permanent state that I call the black apologetic condition.

The challenge here is not to regress into some obscure nativism or race essentialism, as the morally obtuse project of the Native Club tried so clumsily to enforce. Black people now have political power and, by the day, more and more economic power as well. It is how that power is wielded, how the space is occupied, that will determine how fast the imbalances of social and intellectual power can be redressed in our open society.

The man today

And so, the question will be posed now and into the future: is Biko relevant to a post-1994 South Africa? The response I hear often, an appealing one, is that Black Consciousness is relevant as long as white consciousness exists. I understand this reflexive response, as someone recently put it: 'Black man, you are *still* on your own'.

There are two problems with this formulation. First, it suggests that Biko was fixed to a concept of blackness devoid of social context and history. His vision, best expressed in the extraordinary exchange with Judge Boshoff during his trial, was one of 'a very open society' and of black collective action as a platform for being able to speak for oneself, without fear, in the long struggle for such community. In another interview, published in his collected writings (see reference at end of this chapter), he gave substance to this open society; a country in which 'there shall be no minority, there shall be no majority, just the people. And those people will have the same status before the law and they will have the same political rights before the law.' He would argue, in other words, that we have formally attained this status even as the struggle for an equal society continues.

Second, it suggests that race consciousness can end voluntarily, without social intervention. Of course this is unlikely to happen as the deep roots of colonialism and apartheid continue to influence ways of thinking and acting. Another kind of consciousness is required, one based on Biko's vision of an open, egalitarian society.

Power has changed hands since this brilliant 30-year-old was killed by the apartheid state. Yet to this day I am deeply grateful to Steve Biko and his movement for the confidence and self-respect that Black Consciousness engendered in me, and from which basis I felt much more prepared to push back against white racism. Biko remains relevant today to the extent that he inspired a generation of black intellectuals to come into their own and today they occupy positions of considerable influence in this fragile but nevertheless open society.

But I now find myself more attracted towards imagining a world without race, a broader cosmopolitanism, as the sociologist Paul Gilroy calls it, in which one identifies with people on the basis of common citizenship of a troubled world. Yet I do so from the platform of confidence that Black Consciousness bequeathed to me.

Conclusion

On 12 September 2007 I again remembered that gut-wrenching day in 1977 when I heard that my hero had died. I remembered the internal s/urges that committed my young mind also to 'write what I like'. I will recall that it was precisely this sense of pride and self-worth as a black person that made it possible for me to live and lead with confidence in the face of the overwhelming power of whiteness. I also remembered, though, that it is a confidence that today empowers me to join the struggle for a new consciousness about a common identity that defies racial birthmarks or political ideology or national origins.

Note: All the quotations attributed to Biko come from *I Write What I Like*, 2004 Picador Africa, an imprint of Pan Macmillan South Africa, Johannesburg.

Then President of South Africa, Nelson Mandela, unveils a bust of Steve Biko on the 20th anniversary of Biko's death, 12 September 1997.

Courtesy of Benny Gool/Oryx Media Productions/africanpictures.net

13. Achille Mbembe

Biko's testament of hope

Stephen Bantu Biko died 30 years ago. A young black man, he had spent most of his short life thinking about how black people in South Africa could win for themselves a greater degree of intellectual, political and cultural autonomy.

He grew up at a time in South Africa when the physical features associated with blackness (dark skin, kinky hair, full lips) were stigmata of degradation, inferiority and abjection. These were also times when the deadly force of white supremacy denied the rights and severely reduced the life prospects of all blacks.

Like many interpreters of the black condition elsewhere in the world, from the black Americans Frederick Douglass and WEB Du Bois to Frantz Fanon the black revolutionary philosopher from Martinique, Biko realised painfully that whites had refused to accept blacks as fellow citizens. To expect justice from them would be 'naïve,' he argued.

White racism had also engendered a social caste that suffered from self-alienation, he thought. Blacks had been rendered incapable of developing an independent collective identity and had been limited to viewing themselves through the eyes of their oppressors. The truncated consciousness they did possess was suffused with feelings of self-doubt.

Furthermore, these feelings had been internalised through racist propaganda, fear, material want and deprivation, and merciless brutality.

Gradually he came to believe that if they were ever to transcend the vicissitudes of racial bondage and regain faith in their ability blacks should pursue independent collective development and self-reliance through critical self-examination and self-scrutiny.

For him, critical self-examination and self-scrutiny were essential starting points for the development of true self-consciousness and the healing of the wounds inflicted by centuries of racism, degradation and self-estrangement.

During his short life he taught his people to raise their heads above the wasteland of raw, merciless racism and routine humiliation and to stop being afraid.

For black people to learn to be human again, he asked them to look the world straight in the face and to rise above fear, anger and resentment. 'It is fear, he said, that erodes the soul of black people in South Africa.'

Biko never stopped alluding to the 'deeply embedded fear of the black man so prevalent in white society'. Whites, he argued, 'know only too well what exactly they have been doing to blacks'. But 'the tripartite system of fear – that of white fearing the blacks, blacks fearing whites and the government fearing blacks and wishing to allay the fear among whites' made it difficult to build cross-racial coalitions.

He fought hard not only to restore pride to blacks but, even more radically, to destroy the mental shackles by means of which blacks in South Africa had been made to forget that they were fully human. 'The most potent weapon in the hands of the oppressor is the mind of the oppressed,' he used to say. He was convinced that critical introspection could be a powerful tool for reconstructing the humanity of the black person.

He also thought that once this humanity had been restored blacks and whites in South Africa could be open to a different future. But for this to happen whites had to come into consciousness by fighting on their own for their own freedom, in the full knowledge that they could never be free as long as they kept denying freedom to blacks: 'If whites do not like what is happening to the black people, they have the power to stop it here and now,' Biko wrote.

This openness to a new humanity and to a different future is what he meant by 'Black Consciousness'.

In a context in which the possibility of being human was foreclosed for both blacks and whites the concept of 'Black Consciousness' became the name of a different life to come – it was, from the start, a philosophy of life and a philosophy of hope.

Wearied by the long years of black people beating their brains out against the walls of white prejudice, Biko viewed white people with a degree of distrust and suspicion. But ultimately his goal was human brotherhood and sisterhood. He believed that black solidarity would one day make it possible for the members of all races to live together free in one nation. This is why he saw black solidarity as a temporary strategy for realising a political community that fully embodied democratic ideals.

'We do not have the power to subjugate anyone ... Blacks have had enough experience as objects of racism not to wish to turn the tables ... In time we shall be in a position to bestow upon South Africa the greatest gift possible – a more human face'.

Steve Biko walked tall in a land where black men and women were expected to have bent backs. With boldness and bravery he laboured so that South Africa could be made safe for black people.

In the process, he instilled a new spirit of defiance and self-confidence in an entire generation. Ready to sacrifice himself, he feared nobody and nothing. He died strong in body, sturdy in conviction, full of unbending belief, the subject and owner of his death.

He suffered a terrible death at the hands of a grotesque and brutal power – Biko's captive body locked up, tortured, injured, stripped down, chained, the object of mutilation, a human waste that had been utterly disgraced before being lynched.

They wanted his death to be the epitome of indignity and abjection, the symbol of a derisory and superfluous humanity, in the manner of the slave's death.

This is why, in the story of black martyrdom, Biko stands opposite Nelson Mandela, the hero who came up from death and captivity unharmed in body and in mind. Paradoxically, Biko's death only served to illuminate further the permanence of his life. This is why, for as long as history continues, he will be with us.

Since Biko's death blacks in South Africa have secured equal citizenship rights. The constitution outlaws racial discrimination. Today there are significantly more blacks in the middle and upper classes than there were 30 years ago. In the words of a black female entrepreneur, some have more than one luxury vehicle. They own more than one home and can afford private school education for their children, who own cell phones.

'Affirmative action' and 'black economic empowerment' programmes have been designed to improve their socio-economic conditions. Blacks are also more visible than they were 30 years ago in positions of leadership and influence in almost every sector of South African life (government, business, industry, banking and commerce, higher education, media and so on).

The meaning of race and the nature of racial identity are now far more complex and ambiguous than they have ever been. Who is 'black', 'Afrikaner', 'white', 'coloured' or 'Asian' is no longer entirely pre-fixed. The discourses in which South Africans represent race relations are changing.

Notwithstanding the extent of the abuse and daily humiliation of farm workers and tenants in rural areas and small towns, racism itself no longer seems to reside exclusively in the economic and social settings of yesteryear as it migrates into the realm of privately held beliefs.

But the defeat of legalised white supremacy has not meant that the struggle for racial equality is over. Pervasive material inequality between whites and blacks co-exists with formal legal equality. Significant racial inequality remains, for example, in average household income, wealth, home ownership, employment opportunities, and access to quality health care.

The institutional mechanisms for enforcing anti-discriminatory laws are still inadequately administered. Far too many poor blacks are still not in a position where they can create something meaningful with their lives. Too many, still have nothing to lose.

Thus, despite their undeniable progress in some areas, black South Africans are still seeking to realise fully the freedom, equality and prosperity the South African constitution promises.

As we commemorate Biko's death we have to remind ourselves that the moment when South Africa will be able to recognise itself as a truly non-racial community is still far away.

In a country where very few apartheid-era atrocities have been prosecuted, where key political figures refused to testify before the Truth and Reconciliation Commission, where there have been too few acts of public contrition from former executioners, and where most killers and torturers have escaped jail time, the persistent denial of white privilege partly explains the acrimonious nature of race relations. But so does the drive to assert a form of black communal identity predicated on the idea of victimhood.

The two defensive logics of black communal victimhood and white denialism collide and collude, often in unexpected ways. Together, they gradually foster a culture of mutual resentment which, in turn, isolates freedom from responsibility and seriously undermines the prospect of a truly non-racial future. Furthermore, the logic of mutual resentment frustrates blacks' sense of ownership of this country, while foreclosing whites' sense of truly belonging to this place and to this nation.

For Biko's death and its commemoration to have any meaning at all in our time we need to keep asking some of the most difficult questions he himself asked in his life time, or those he would probably ask today:

- What could Black Consciousness possibly entail today, in a free South Africa?
- Is black solidarity still essential to achieve the full freedom and equality the South African constitution promises?
- Is the model of black radical politics advocated by Biko still adequate to address the problems South Africa in general, and blacks in particular, face today, or should most of the ideas commonly associated with this tradition be rethought?
- In particular, we have to ask ourselves whether 'race' (and the forms of solidarity it may sustain) can still be taken as a sound basis for social identities, cultural affiliations, membership of associations, public policy, or political movements; or whether any form of racial particularism is needlessly divisive.

- How can we re-invigorate the dream of racial reconciliation and re-activate the possibilities of cross-racial solidarities as the basis for progressive and radical political practice here and now?
- What further demands should we make on ourselves as citizens and on the state for racial reform if racial justice has not yet been achieved?
- Are the core values of the Black Consciousness Movement such as equal citizenship for all persons; respect for individual autonomy; democratic constitutional government under the rule of law; the basic rights to freedom of conscience, expression and association; tolerance for different concepts of good; equal opportunity in education and employment; and a guaranteed minimum standard of living compatible with the core values of a democratic, liberal and constitutional state.
- If Black Consciousness is to be sustained in a post-1994 era which of the ideas commonly associated with that tradition will have to be re-thought?
- Is Black Consciousness the same as 'black economic empowerment or is the ideology of 'black economic empowerment' the new way in which the 'black elite' advances its narrow interests and legitimates its hegemony over the black working class and the black poor?

In order to address these questions it might help to remind ourselves that Biko defended a concept of blackness, or of black solidarity, that was not concerned primarily with questions of identity but urged a commitment to defeating racism, to eliminating unjust racial inequalities, and to improving the life prospects of those racialised as blacks.

Blacks, for him, were 'those who are by law or tradition politically, economically and socially discriminated against as a group in the South African society'. They were also those who identified themselves as 'a unit in the struggle towards the realisation of their aspirations'.

To be black was 'not a matter of pigmentation', it was a 'reflection of a mental attitude'. To describe oneself as black, he argued, was 'to set oneself on the road towards emancipation'.

The term 'black' was discriminatory and Biko himself said that it was 'not necessarily all-inclusive'. For him, to not be white did not necessarily mean to be black: 'If one's aspiration is whiteness but his pigmentation makes attainment of this impossible, then that person is a non-white. Any man who calls a white man "Baas", any man who serves in the police force or Security Branch is ipso facto a non-white. Black people – real black people – are those who can manage to hold their heads high in defiance rather than willingly surrender their souls to the white man.'

By defining blackness in these terms he dispensed with the idea of race as a biological essence while continuing to embrace blackness as an emancipatory weapon.

His concern for blacks as a racialised subordinated group did not mean an endorsement of an exacerbated sense of victimisation and disempowerment. Indeed, the difference between 'Black Consciousness' and 'nativism' is that. in the name of the right to self-definition, 'nativism' paradoxically recreates and consolidates the mental ghetto – a lethal device white racism used so effectively in order to inflict maximum psychic damage on the soul of black folks.

Contrary to Black Consciousness, nativism always tends to repeat the sorry history it pretends to redress. It is, in essence, a self-defeating attitude.

Black Consciousness, on the other hand, belongs to the old and enduring tradition of black nationalism. Black nationalism is an old, but thoroughly modern political tradition which emerged in the 19th century in response to contexts in which, regarded as inherently inferior and thereby incapable of self-government, blacks were oppressed on account of their blackness.

In such contexts black nationalism became an expression of the desire of blacks to escape the suffering caused by racial injustice and to live in a just society in which they would be able to rule themselves and shape their own destinies, while being in control of their own institutions.

Black nationalism, in this sense, was the result of a mutual recognition of black people's common vulnerability to white domination and their collective resolve to overcome it.

Traditionally, black nationalists advocate such things as black self-determination, racial solidarity and group self-reliance, various forms of voluntary racial separation, pride in the historic achievements of persons of African descent, a concerted effort to overcome racial self-hate and to instil black self-love, militant collective resistance to white supremacy, the development and preservation of a distinctive black cultural identity, and the recognition of Africa as the true homeland of those who are racially black.

Our situation today is somewhat different from that in Biko's day. For instance, a major revision of South Africa's white supremacist ideology is under way.

Today, white supremacy is no longer a matter of asserting the 'natural inferiority' of blacks. The assault is no longer on the idea of a common humanity, a world of individuals endowed with common rights. Instead, the defence of racial inequality and stratification is articulated in three new ways.

First, it assumes the form of a contest over the moral legitimacy and appropriateness of policies of redress. Here the belief is that law should neither mandate social equality nor attempt to eradicate conditions of racial inequality and the legacy of past victimisation.

Second, the apology of racial inequality is gradually couched in the rhetoric of rights, fairness and equality. Such rhetoric is mobilised in an effort to institutionalise racial privilege that is trying to mask its racial nature. By denying the fact that past racial injustices can be rectified by legally enforced and race-conscious remedies in the present it is hoped that real differences among racial groups will be protected and preserved and the imperative of justice and redress indefinitely postponed.

Third, for many beneficiaries of past racial atrocities, reconciliation means that blacks should forget about South Africa's fractured past and move on. Furthermore, many whites have not only retreated to a comfortable position of personal non-culpability, many now believe that white racism can no longer be considered the most fundamental cause of black poverty. Nor can it be held responsible any longer for the troubling gaps in life-chances between black South Africans and their white compatriots.

The transformation of white supremacist ideology notwithstanding, we have to be able to respond to today's tough moral and political questions:

- Is 'black empowerment' or 'transformation' a form of reparation and redress or, rather, a temporary expedient that will at some point wither away?

- can injustice rendered in the past against a black person be compensated for by discriminating against a white in the present?
- Do claims for racial redress advanced by former victims of racial discrimination irremediably compromise the non-racist principles enshrined in the constitution?

A distinctive mark of black nationalism has always been the politicisation of black peoplehood and one of the distinctive contributions of the Black Consciousness Movement to the theory of black nationalism is its insistence on moral sovereignty.

In Biko's political language moral sovereignty encompassed the three areas of social equality and democratic citizenship, self-government and self-representation, and autonomous thinking.

In those three areas South Africa still has a long way to go. To be sure, today, black South Africans enjoy the right of self-government. They are their own rulers. But whether each individual South African embodies the essential ingredients of the sovereign moral principle which, for Biko, comprises the true basis of liberty, is open to question.

Clearly, if citizenship is more than the right to vote, South Africa has to attend to the unfinished business of democracy.

This implies, for instance, a profound reform of the electoral law and the abolition of the practice of floor crossing. The people as a whole should regain the right to elect their president. As in every other major democracy, Members of Parliament and other representative bodies should be elected by their constituencies and should be accountable to the latter.

And for blacks to have true social equality with whites, they have to match whites in cultural and economic achievement.

Without proportionate black and white attainment in the central spheres of life the two races will not truly live together on terms of mutual respect and dignity. The commitment to substantive, rather than merely formal, equality should therefore form the backbone of South African efforts to build a truly democratic society.

As far as autonomous thinking is concerned, it does not simply mean that blacks should not allow whites, even those sympathetic to black interests, to think for them; it means nobody should allow anybody else to think for him or her. Not only should blacks resist white paternalism, they should also resist black paternalism. Independence of mind was not only crucial under conditions of domination, it is an essential resource in the practice of freedom and the fight for equality.

Furthermore, black solidarity cannot mean communal nationalism, a form of authoritarian collectivism which consists in the belief that all black people should act unanimously under the leadership of a 'big man'. Communal nationalism also tends to reduce all forms of black disadvantage to racial oppression or white supremacy.

Communal nationalists believe that our task here and today is still to defeat white supremacy. To that effect, they argue that we must close ranks.

But racism is not the only significant obstacle black South Africans now face. The social and political changes the country has undergone since 1994 have significantly shifted the context of black political struggles.

Today, blacks in South Africa have political power. Their ability to effect meaningful social changes is substantive. They can no longer act as if they were totally powerless. For black solidarity to serve as a political and moral resource in the post- liberation era it needs to be refined not only to deal with new social realities but, even more importantly, to conform better to democratic principles.

For black solidarity to remain the moral struggle it was in times of bondage it must be rooted in a commitment to equal justice for all – a commitment to enable all voices to be heard, and to protect the legitimate interests of minorities. Without such protections majoritarianism will remain a menacing force, capable not only of restricting freedom but of undermining the prospects for non-racialism itself.

The burden of racial oppression has been formally lifted. The great challenge today is how to put in place a radical programme for black upliftment and, in so doing, how to achieve economic justice within a market-dominated economy.

To achieve a modicum of social justice after apartheid was abolished and racial segregation outlawed South Africa had to dismantle the barriers that were erected against full justice for all and attend to distributional inequalities.

For black South Africans in particular, freedom has to translate into an expanded control over their labour and their lives. It is the role of the state to galvanise them as they struggle to eradicate the legacies of the violence that preyed on their vulnerabilities during the years of captivity.

But economic justice will not be achieved if blacks do not realise that they must rely on themselves, as individuals and as a collective, in their effort to rise above their low position in South African society.

The surest road to a dignified existence is self-respect, self-help, independence of mind, creativity and ambition.

The transformation project can easily turn into social quackery if its first goal is not to restore capacities to those who have been deprived of these by unjust laws and racist policies.

Morally bankrupt as it was, something can be learnt from the Afrikaner model of empowerment (*reddingsdaad*). To a large extent, this was a social movement and not simply a state-inspired initiative. It is significant that it was an economic movement with intellectual and cultural foundations. In order to foster their economic upliftment the Afrikaners created two structures: the Federale Volksbelegging (Federal People's Investment) and the Reddingsdaadbond.

The role of these two institutions was to mobilise capital, to pool the financial resources of white Afrikaans commercial farmers, entrepreneurs, and workers in order to regain control of their savings, labour and buying power while promoting self-help at various levels, including language, culture and politics.

That is how almost every Afrikaner came to have something at stake in the future of South Africa – a home, a job, education, something they were ready to fight for and to protect.

A meaningful class differentiation among black people is emerging in South Africa, the long-term significance of which cannot be downplayed. Because of growing differences in education, income, occupation and opportunity, there will inevitably be a more advantaged group within the black population whose material interests might diverge from those of their more disadvantaged racial kin.

Today, we have a proud new black elite based on education, income, occupational status, political connections and, eventually, cultural capital. But, for a number of critics, the kind of black economic empowerment pursued by the government and white capital is less than a policy, it is a method perfected by the oligarchy to placate the political elites and to buy protection.

What is emerging is an unproductive, comprador class of rich black politicians and ex-politicians who depend on white capital and entertain a parasitic relationship with the government.

On the other extreme, racialised poverty is exacerbated. A vast urban black underclass is in the making – a mass of disposable people who have nothing to lose, many of whom depend on handouts from the government in the name of 'service delivery'.

A radical programme of black upliftment is urgently needed in order to avoid the trap of 'service delivery'. The philosophical premise of such a radical programme should be self-help, its goal to create self-reliant individuals.

There is a long tradition of self-help in the history of black thought, a tradition that has always placed a strong emphasis not only on the kind of education that will prepare the black poor to enter the workforce and to undertake entrepreneurial endeavours, but has also placed a significant importance on the cultivation of a sense of personal responsibility.

According to this tradition, each black person should take primary responsibility for her or his condition. Blacks should not view themselves as victims, nor should they encourage others to look upon them as such. Among the virtues to be cultivated should be the willingness to make sacrifices in the short term for greater gains in the future.

The other component of this self-help philosophy has always been institution-building for purposes of racial upliftment. This is a tradition that has always put a premium on institution-building and self-organisation as the true road to freedom and has encouraged blacks to save and invest rather than to spend money on entertainment and luxury goods.

For instance Jamaican-born Marcus Garvey, leader of the back-to-Africa campaign of the early 1900s, was an exponent of black self-help and championed capitalism as the road to black liberation. He believed that the development of black businesses on a global scale would ultimately lead whites to respect blacks and to deal with them on equal terms.

None of this should mean the encouragement of self-segregation. The goal of black solidarity and black economic assertion should always be to deepen South Africa's democracy. That is where its emancipatory potential lies.

Historically, it is a fact that formerly oppressed groups have advanced mainly through self-organisation. But black solidarity cannot help democracy if it remains but an embrace of the horn of racial particularism.

No re-assessment of Biko's legacy can proceed today as if our age was not an age of contradictions, the biggest of which is probably the simultaneity of massive social mobility and the ubiquity of death in our lives.

To a large extent, to die on the way up is the single most political dilemma of our times. The overwhelming presence of death in black people's everyday life only serves to dramatise the predicament of freedom in South Africa. Weekly funerals have become the dominant way in which time is remembered – death on the road, death on a train, random death at the hands of criminals, death from tuberculosis and malnutrition, and more and more cases of suicide in the townships and the squatter camps.

If South Africa is to become a society that fosters cross-racial solidarity as the basis of progressive and radical politics for our time, blacks cannot be content to celebrate blackness in much the same way as white supremacists do whiteness. Nor should black solidarity embrace racial particularism, nativism, communal nationalism or the politics of difference for the sake of difference.

If black solidarity is to serve as a political resource in the broader quest for life and racial justice, it must be firmly rooted in a moral commitment to racial reconciliation and equal justice for all. Only such a commitment can enable South Africa to become an Afropolitan nation in which race as such is no longer the basis for modern African nationality.

Freedom for black South Africans will be meaningless if it does not entail a commitment to freedom for every African, black or white.

Furthermore, if black and white South Africans are to be respected in the world, their original homeland, Africa, must be regenerated. The project of African redemption and restoration has been at the core of black thought since 1860.

Biko himself believed that a 'great gift' was still to come from Africa. 'The great powers of the world may have done wonders in giving the world an industrial and military look, but the great gift still has to come from Africa – giving the world a more human face.'

Because of its history, South Africa has an opportunity unique in the history of humankind to be the first nation on Earth to finally untie the knot of race. In doing so, this nation will open the door for a politics of life. And at last, Africa will give the world the human face the world deserves.

Biko at the East London airport in 1977.

Courtesy of Peter Bruce.

14.

Steve Biko

Black Consciousness and the quest for a true humanity

It is perhaps fitting to start by examining why it is necessary for us to think collectively about a problem we never created. In doing so, I do not wish to concern myself unnecessarily with the white people of South Africa, but to get to the right answers, we must ask the right questions; we have to find out what went wrong – where and when; and we have to find out whether our position is a deliberate creation of God or an artificial fabrication of the truth by power-hungry people whose motive is authority, security, wealth and comfort. In other words, the 'Black Consciousness' approach would be irrelevant in a colourless and non-exploitative egalitarian society. It is relevant here because we believe that an anomalous situation is a deliberate creation of man.

There is no doubt that the colour question in South African politics was originally introduced for economic reasons. The leaders of the white community had to create some kind of barrier between black and white so that the whites could enjoy privileges at the expense of blacks and still feel free to give a moral justification for the obvious exploitation that pricked even the hardest of white consciences. However, tradition has it that whenever a group of people has tasted the lovely fruits of wealth, security and prestige it begins to find it more comfortable to believe in the obvious lie and to accept it as normal that it alone is entitled to privilege. In order to believe this seriously, it needs to convince itself of all the arguments that support the lie. It is not surprising, therefore, that in South Africa, after generations of exploitation, white people on the whole have come to believe in the inferiority of the black man, so much so that while the race problem started as an offshoot of the economic greed exhibited by white people, it has now become a serious problem on its own. White people now despise black people, not because they need to reinforce their attitude and so justify their position of privilege but simply because they actually believe that black is inferior and bad. This is the basis upon which whites are working in South Africa, and it is what makes South African society racist.

The racism we meet does not only exist on an individual basis; it is also institutionalised to make it look like the South African way of life. Although of late there has been a feeble attempt to gloss over the overt racist elements in the system, it is still true that the system derives its nourishment from the existence of anti-black attitudes in society. To make the lie live even longer, blacks have to be denied any chance of accidentally proving their equality with white men. For this reason there is job reservation, lack of training in skilled work, and a tight orbit around professional possibilities for blacks. Stupidly enough, the system turns back to say that blacks are inferior because they have no economists, no engineers, etc., although it is made impossible for blacks to acquire these skills.

To give authenticity to their lie and to show the righteousness of their claim, whites have further worked out detailed schemes to 'solve' the racial situation in this country. Thus, a pseudo-parliament has been created for 'Coloureds', and several 'Bantu states' are in the process of being set up. So independent and fortunate are they that they do not have to spend a cent on their defence because they have nothing to fear from white South Africa which will always come to their assistance in times of need. One does not, of course, fail to see the arrogance of whites and their contempt for blacks, even in their well-considered modern schemes for subjugation.

The overall success of the white power structure has been in managing to bind the whites together in defence of the status quo. By skilfully playing on that imaginary bogey – *swart gevaar* – they have managed to convince even diehard liberals that there is something to fear in the idea of the black man assuming his rightful place at the helm of the South African ship. Thus after years of silence we are able to hear the familiar voice of Alan Paton[1] saying, as far away as London: 'Perhaps apartheid is worth a try'. 'At whose expense, Dr. Paton?', asks an intelligent black journalist. Hence whites in general reinforce each other even though they allow some moderate disagreements on the details of subjugation schemes. There is no doubt that they do not question the validity of white values. They see nothing anomalous in the fact that they alone are arguing about the future of 17 million blacks – in a land which is the natural backyard of the black people. Any proposals for change emanating from the black world are viewed with great indignation. Even the so-called Opposition, the United Party, has the nerve to tell the Coloured people that they are asking for too much. A journalist from a liberal newspaper like *The Sunday Times* of Johannesburg describes a black student – who is only telling the truth – as a militant, impatient young man.

It is not enough for whites to be on the offensive. So immersed are they in prejudice that they do not believe that blacks can formulate their thoughts without white guidance and trusteeship. Thus, even those whites who see much wrong with the system make it their business to control the response of the blacks to the provocation. No one is suggesting that it is not the business of liberal whites to oppose what is wrong. However, it appears to us as too much of a coincidence that liberals – few as they are – should not only be determining the *modus operandi* of those blacks who oppose the system, but also leading it, in spite of their involvement in the system. To us it seems that their role spells out the totality of the white power structure – the fact that though whites are our problem, it is still other whites who want to tell us how to deal with that problem. They do so by dragging all sorts of red herrings across our paths. They tell us that the situation is a class struggle rather than a racial one. Let them go to Van Tonder in the Free State and tell him this. We believe we know what the problem is, and we will stick by our findings.

I want to go a little deeper in this discussion because it is time we killed this false political coalition between blacks and whites as long as it is set up on a wrong analysis of our situation. I want to kill it for another reason – namely that it forms at present the greatest stumbling block to our unity. It dangles before freedom-hungry blacks promises of a great future for which no one in these groups seems to be working particularly hard.

The basic problem in South Africa has been analysed by liberal whites as being apartheid. They argue that in order to oppose it we have to form non-racial groups. Between these two extremes, they claim, lies the land of milk and honey for which we are working. The *thesis*, the *anti-thesis* and the *synthesis* have been mentioned by some great philosophers as the cardinal points around which any social revolution revolves. For the liberals, the *thesis* is apartheid, the *antithesis* is non-racialism, but the synthesis is very feebly defined. They want to tell the blacks that they see integration as the ideal solution. Black Consciousness defines the situation differently. The *thesis* is in fact a strong white racism and therefore, the *antithesis* to this must, ipso facto, be a strong solidarity amongst the blacks on whom this white racism seeks to prey. Out of these two situations we can therefore hope to reach some kind of balance – a true humanity where power politics will have no place. This analysis spells out the difference between the old and new approaches. The failure of the liberals is in fact that their *antithesis* is already a watered-down version of the truth whose close proximity to the thesis will nullify the purported balance. This accounts for the failure of the Sprocas[2] commissions to make any real headway, for they are already looking for an 'alternative' acceptable to the white man. Everybody in the commissions knows what is right but all are looking for the most seemly way of dodging the responsibility of saying what is right.

It is much more important for blacks to see this difference than it is for whites. We must learn to accept that no group, however benevolent, can ever hand power to the vanquished on a plate. We must accept that the limits of tyrants are prescribed by the endurance of those whom they oppress. As long as we go to Whitey begging cap in hand for our own emancipation, we are giving him further sanction to continue with his racist and oppressive system. We must realise that our situation is not a mistake on the part of whites but a deliberate act, and that no amount of moral lecturing will persuade the white man to 'correct' the situation. The system concedes nothing without demand, for it formulates its very method of operation on the basis that the ignorant will learn to know, the child will grow into an adult and therefore demands will begin to be made. It gears itself to resist demands in whatever way it sees fit. When you refuse to make these demands and choose to come to a round table to beg for your deliverance, you are asking for the contempt of those who have power over you. This is why we must reject the beggar tactics that are being forced on us by those who wish to appease our cruel masters. This is where the SASO message and cry 'Black man, you are on your own!' becomes relevant.

The concept of integration, whose virtues are often extolled in white liberal circles, is full of unquestioned assumptions that embrace white values. It is a concept long defined by whites and never examined by blacks. It is based on the assumption that all is well with the system apart from some degree of mismanagement by irrational conservatives at the top. Even the people who argue for integration often forget to veil it in its supposedly beautiful covering. They tell each other that, were it not for job reservation, there would be a beautiful market to exploit . They forget they are talking about people. They see blacks as additional levers to some complicated industrial machines. This is white man's integration – an integration based on exploitative values. It is an integration in which black will compete with black, using each other as rungs up a step ladder leading them to white values. It is an integration in which the black man will have to prove himself in terms of these values before meriting acceptance and ultimate assimilation, and in which the poor will grow poorer and the rich richer in a country where the poor have always been black. We do not want to be reminded that it is we, the indigenous people, who are poor and exploited in the land of our birth. These are concepts which the Black Consciousness approach wishes to eradicate from the black man's mind before our society is driven to chaos by irresponsible people from Coca-cola and hamburger cultural backgrounds.

Black Consciousness is an attitude of mind and a way of life, the most positive call to emanate from the black world for a long time. Its essence is the realisation by the black man of the need to rally together with his brothers around the cause of their oppression – the blackness of their skin – and to operate as a group to rid themselves of the shackles that bind them to perpetual servitude. It is based on a self-examination which has ultimately led them to believe that by seeking to run away from themselves and emulate the white man, they are insulting the intelligence of whoever created them black. The philosophy of Black Consciousness therefore expresses group pride and the determination of the black to rise and attain the envisaged self. Freedom is the ability to define oneself with one's possibilities held back not by the power of other people over one but only by one's relationship to God and to natural surroundings. On his own, therefore, the black man wishes to explore his surroundings and test his possibilities – in other words to make his freedom real by whatever means he deems fit. At the heart of this kind of thinking is the realisation by blacks that the most potent weapon in the hands of the oppressor is the mind of the oppressed. If one is free at heart, no man-made chains can bind one to servitude, but if one's mind is so manipulated and controlled by the oppressor as to make the oppressed believe that he is a liability to the white man, then there will be nothing the oppressed can do to scare his powerful masters. Hence thinking along lines of Black Consciousness makes the black man see himself as a being complete in himself. It makes him less dependent and more free to express his manhood. At the end of it all he cannot tolerate attempts by anybody to dwarf the significance of his manhood.

In order that Black Consciousness can be used to advantage as a philosophy to apply to people in a position like ours, a number of points have to be observed. As people existing in a continuous struggle for truth, we have to examine and question old concepts, values and systems. Having found the right answers we shall then work for consciousness among all people to make it possible for us to proceed towards putting these answers into effect. In this process, we have to evolve our own schemes, forms and strategies to suit the need and situation, always keeping in mind our fundamental beliefs and values.

In all aspects of the black-white relationship, now and in the past, we see a constant tendency by whites to depict blacks as of an inferior status. Our culture, our history and indeed all aspects of the black man's life have been battered nearly out of shape in the great collision between the indigenous values and the Anglo-Boer culture.

The first people to come and relate to blacks in a human way in South Africa were the missionaries. They were in the vanguard of the colonisation movement to 'civilise and educate' the savages and introduce the Christian message to them. The religion they brought was quite foreign to the black indigenous people. African religion in its essence was not radically different from Christianity. We also believe in one God, we had our own community of saints through whom we related to our God, and we did not find it compatible with our way of life to worship God in isolation from the various aspects of our lives. Hence worship was not a specialised function that found expression once a week in a secluded building, but rather it featured in our wars, our beer-drinking, our dances and our customs in general. Whenever Africans drank they would first relate to God by giving a portion of their beer away as a token of thanks. When anything went wrong at home they would offer sacrifice to God to appease him and atone for their sins. There was no hell in our religion. We believed in the inherent goodness of man – hence we took it for granted that all people at death joined the community of saints and therefore merited our respect.

It was the missionaries who confused the people with their new religion. They scared our people with stories of hell. They painted their God as a demanding God who wanted worship 'or else'. People had to discard their clothes and their customs in order to be accepted in this new religion. Knowing how religious the African people were, the missionaries stepped up their terror campaign on the emotions of the people with their detailed accounts of eternal burning, tearing of hair and gnashing of teeth. By some strange and twisted logic, they argued that theirs was a scientific religion and ours a superstition – all this in spite of the biological discrepancy which is at the base of their religion. This cold and cruel religion was strange to the indigenous people and caused frequent strife between the converted and the 'pagans', for the former, having imbibed the false values from white society, were taught to ridicule and despise those who defended the truth of their indigenous religion. With the ultimate acceptance of the western religion down went our cultural values!

While I do not wish to question the basic truth at the heart of the Christian message, there is a strong case for a re-examination of Christianity. It has proven a very adaptable religion which does not seek to supplement existing orders but – like any universal truth – to find application within a particular situation. More than anyone else, the missionaries knew that not all they did was essential to the spread of the message. But the basic intention went much further than merely spreading the word. Their arrogance and their monopoly on truth, beauty and moral judgment taught them to despise native customs and traditions and to seek to infuse their own new values into these societies.

Here then we have the case for Black Theology. While not wishing to discuss Black Theology at length, let it suffice to say that it seeks to relate God and Christ once more to the black man and his daily problems. It wants to describe Christ as a fighting God, not a passive God who allows a lie to rest unchallenged. It grapples with existential problems and does not claim to be a theology of absolutes. It seeks to bring back God to the black man and to the truth and reality of his situation. This is an important aspect of Black Consciousness, for quite a large proportion of black people in South Africa are Christians still swimming in a mire of confusion – the aftermath of the missionary approach. It is the duty therefore of all black priests and ministers of religion to save Christianity by adopting Black Theology's approach and thereby once more uniting the black man with his God.

A long look should also be taken at the educational system for blacks. The same tense situation was found as long ago as the arrival of the missionaries. Children were taught, under the pretext of hygiene, good manners and other such vague concepts, to despise their mode of upbringing at home and to question the values and customs of their society. The result was the expected one – children and parents saw life differently and the former lost respect for the latter. Now in African society it is a cardinal sin for a child to lose respect for his parent. Yet how can one prevent the loss of respect between child and parent when the child is taught by his know-all white tutors to disregard his family teachings? Who can resist losing respect for his tradition when in school his whole culture background is summed up in one word – barbarism?

Thus we can immediately see the logic of placing the missionaries in the forefront of the colonisation process. A man who succeeds in making a group of people accept a foreign concept in which he is expert makes them perpetual students whose progress in the particular field can only be evaluated by him; the student must constantly turn to him for guidance and promotion. In being forced to accept the Anglo-Boer culture, the blacks have allowed themselves to be at the mercy of the white man and to have him as their eternal supervisor. Only he can tell us how good our performance is and instinctively each of us is at pains to please this powerful, all-knowing master. This is what Black Consciousness seeks to eradicate.

As one black writer says, colonialism is never satisfied with having the native in its grip but, by some strange logic, it must turn to his past and disfigure and distort it. Hence the history of the black man in this country is most disappointing to read. It is presented merely as a long succession of defeats. The Xhosas were thieves who went to war for stolen property; the Boers never provoked the Xhosas but merely went on 'punitive expeditions' to teach the thieves a lesson. Heroes like Makana3 who were essentially revolutionaries are painted as superstitious trouble-makers who lied to the people about bullets turning into water. Great nation-builders like Shaka are cruel tyrants who frequently attacked smaller tribes for no reason but for some sadistic purpose. Not only is there no objectivity in the history taught us but there is frequently an appalling misrepresentation of facts that sicken even the uninformed student.

Thus a lot of attention has to be paid to our history if we as blacks want to aid each other in our coming into consciousness. We have to rewrite our history and produce in it the heroes that formed the core of our resistance to the white invaders. More has to be revealed, and stress has to be laid on the successful nation building attempts of men such as Shaka, Moshoeshoe and Hintsa. These areas call for intense research to provide some sorely-needed missing links. We would be too naive to expect our conquerors to write unbiased histories about us but we have to destroy the myth that our history starts in 1652, the year Van Riebeeck landed at the Cape.

Our culture must be defined in concrete terms. We must relate the past to the present and demontrate a historical evolution of the modern black man. There is a tendency to think of our culture as a static culture that was arrested in 1652 and has never developed since. The 'return to the bush' concept suggests that we have nothing to boast of except lions, sex and drink. We accept that when colonisation sets in it devours the indigenous culture and leaves behind a bastard culture that may thrive at the pace allowed it by the dominant culture. But we also have to realise that the basic tenets of our culture have largely succeeded in withstanding the process of bastardisation and that even at this moment we can still demonstrate that we appreciate a man for himself. Ours is a true man-centred society whose sacred tradition is that of sharing. We must reject, as we have been doing, the individualistic cold approach to life that is the cornerstone of the Anglo-Boer culture. We must seek to restore to the black man the great importance we used to give to human relations, the high regard for people and their property and for life in general; to reduce the triumph of technology over man and the materialistic element that is slowly creeping into our society.

These are essential features of our black culture to which we must cling. Black culture above all implies freedom on our part to innovate without recourse to white values. This innovation is part of the natural development of any culture. A culture is essentially the society's composite answer to the varied problems of life. We are experiencing every day and whatever we do adds to the richness of our cultural heritage as long as it has man as its centre. The adoption of black theatre and drama is one such important innovation which we need to encourage and to develop. We know that our love of music and rhythm has relevance even in this day.

Being part of an exploitative society in which we are often the direct objects of exploitation, we need to evolve a strategy towards our economic situation. We are aware that the blacks are still colonised even within the borders of South Africa. Their cheap labour has helped to make South Africa what it is today. Our money from the townships takes a one-way journey to white shops and white banks, and all we do in our lives is pay the white man either with labour or in coin. Capitalistic exploitative tendencies, coupled with the overt arrogance of white racism, have conspired against us. Thus in South Africa now it is very expensive to be poor. It is the poor people who stay furthest from town and therefore have to spend more money on transport to come and work for white people; it is the poor people who use uneconomic and inconvenient fuel like paraffin and coal because of the refusal of the white man to install electricity in black areas; it is the poor people who are governed by many ill-defined restrictive laws and therefore have to spend money on fines for 'technical' offences; it is the poor people who have no hospitals and are therefore exposed to exorbitant charges by private doctors; it is the poor people who use untarred roads, have to walk long distances, and therefore experience the greatest wear and tear on commodities like shoes; it is the poor people who have to pay for their children's books while whites get them free. It does not need to be said that it is the black people who are poor.

We therefore need to take another look at how best to use our economic power, little as it may seem to be. We must seriously examine the possibilities of establishing business co-operatives whose interests will be ploughed back into community development programmes. We should think along such lines as the 'buy black' campaign once suggested in Johannesburg and establish our own banks for the benefit of the community. Organisational development amongst blacks has only been low because we have allowed it to be. Now that we are on our own, it is an absolute duty for us to fulfil these needs.

The last step in Black Consciousness is to broaden the base of our operation. One of the basic tenets of Black Consciousness is totality of involvement. This means that all blacks must sit as one big unit, and no fragmentation and distraction from the mainstream of events be allowed. Hence we must resist the attempts by protagonists of the Bantustan theory to fragment our approach. We are oppressed not as individuals, not as Zulus, Xhosas, Vendas or Indians. We are oppressed because we are black. We must use that very concept to unite ourselves and to respond as a cohesive group. We must cling to each other with a tenacity that will shock the perpetrators of evil.

Our preparedness to take upon ourselves the cudgels of the struggle will see us through. We must remove from our vocabulary completely the concept of fear. Truth must ultimately triumph over evil, and the white man has always nourished his greed on this basic fear that shows itself in the black community. Special Branch agents will not turn the lie into truth, and one must ignore them. In a true bid for change we have to take off our coats, be prepared to lose our comfort and security, our jobs and positions of prestige, and our families, for just as it is true that 'leadership and security are basically incompatible', a struggle without casualties is no struggle. We must realise that prophetic cry of black students: 'Black man, you are on your own!'

Some will charge that we are racist but these people are using exactly the values we reject. We do not have the power to subjugate anyone. We are merely responding to provocation in the most realistic possible way. Racism does not only imply exclusion of one race by another – it always pre-supposes that the exclusion is for the purposes of subjugation. Blacks have had enough experience as objects of racism not to wish to turn the tables. While it may be relevant now to talk about black in relation to white, we must not make this our preoccupation, for it can be a negative exercise. As we proceed further towards the achievement of our goals let us talk more about ourselves and our struggle and less about whites.

We have set out on a quest for true humanity, and somewhere on the distant horizon we can see the glittering prize. Let us march forth with courage and determination, drawing strength from our common plight and our brotherhood. In time we shall be in a position to bestow upon South Africa the greatest gift possible – a more human face.

1   One of the leaders of the South African Liberal Party of the 1950s, and author of the classic *Cry the Beloved Country*.
2   Sprocas stands for Study Project on Christianity in an Apartheid Society. It was set up by the South African Council of Churches and the Christian Institute in 1968.
3   Early 19th century Xhosa prophet sentenced to life imprisonment on Robben Island and drowned while escaping in a boat. Refusal by blacks to accept the truth of his death led to the mythical hope of his eventual return.

Ntsiki Biko attending a re-enactment of Biko's funeral, King William's Town, 2007.

Courtesy of Michael Pinyana, *Daily Dispatch*, Johnnic Communications.

Contributors

Darryl Accone is Books Editor of the *Mail & Guardian* and teaches African Cinema, and Writing for Non-Fiction and Fiction in the School of Arts at the University of the Witwatersrand, Johannesburg. As a scholar, Accone explores the Chinese diaspora, and the neglected ideas of Guy Debord, particularly as set out in Debord's *The Society of the Spectacle*. Among his recent publications is 'Ghost People: Localising the Chinese Self in an African context' (*Asian Studies Review* 30(3), 2006). He is a Fellow of the Salzburg Seminar in Austria and of the International Writers Workshop of Hong Kong Baptist University, where he spent a month-long residency in December 2004. Accone's writing includes non-fiction, memoir and fiction. His book *All Under Heaven: The Story of a Chinese family in South Africa* (David Philip) was short-listed for the 2005 Alan Paton Award.

Zithulele Cindi, ccurrently Executive Director of Unity Incorporation, the custodian of sustainable development funds in South Africa, and National Chairman of the Azanian People's Organisation (Azapo), was born in 1950 in Alexandra Township. Cindi matriculated at Orlando West High School Soweto where he was briefly active in the affairs of the African Student Movement, later to become the South African Student Movement. He joined the Black People's Convention in 1972 and has been active since then in various positions within the Black Consciousness Movement. More than 21 years in trades unions influence his current work at Unity Incorporation. He is a labour representative on the board of the National Productivity Institute and serves as chairman of the Productivity Awards Committee. He is a board member of the African Institute for Corporate Citizenship and the Industrial Ministry and a member of the African Task Force on Sustainable Banking and Financial Initiatives.

Saths Cooper, a graduate of UNISA, Wits, and Boston University, where he obtained his PhD in Clinical/Community Psychology as a Fulbright Scholar, is vice-president of the International Union of Psychological Science. He taught at Wits, Boston and the University of the Western Cape (UWC). A close colleague of Steve Biko, Cooper played a key role in the anti-apartheid struggle and was banned, house arrested and jailed for nine years. He is a Life Fellow of the International Biographical Centre in Cambridge (UK), Deputy Governor of the American Biographical Institute and was the first National Director of the Institute for Multi-Party Democracy. He served on the councils of Wits and Durban Westville and was the last Vice-Chancellor and Principal of the UDW before it was merged in UKZN.

Duncan Innes is a facilitator and expert in labour relations. He consults widely to trade unions, employers and government, was formerly a professor at Wits University and is the author of more than 60 publications. Born in Cape Town, he lived there until he went to England in 1972. During a visit to Cape Town in 1980, he was detained for a month in Caledon Square Police station because of his involvement in anti-apartheid work in the UK. He returned to South Africa in 1981.

Jonathan Jansen was born in Montagu in the rural Western Cape, raised on the Cape Flats, taught high school science in Vredenburg and District Six and left South Africa in 1985 to study for a Master's degree in science education at Cornell University in the USA. He returned in 1991 after completing a doctorate at Stanford University. He worked with non-governmental organisations from his base in Johannesburg before taking his first academic job as a professor of curriculum studies at the then University of Durban Westville. He is Dean of the Faculty of Education at the University of Pretoria. In October 2007 Jansen travelled to Stanford University in the USA where he is Fulbright scholar, completing a book on 'The Politics of Memory in South Africa', examining how white South African students remember and enact the past. His recent books include: *Patterns of Desegregation in White Working Class Schools* (with Saloshna Vandeyar, University Press of America, 2008) and *On Second Thoughts*, a collection of writings (2007, Actua Press).

Bokwe Mafuna was born in Mafikeng in 1937 where he began his schooling at St Mary's Mission School, moving on to St Eugen's College, near Cyferbult. He left school at the age of 15, moved to Johannesburg and worked as a labourer. In 1961, he joined a Catholic seminary, studied for four years to become a priest but later became a trade unionist and, eventually, a journalist on the *Rand Daily Mail*. After meeting Steve Biko, Mafuna became active in the BCM, worked for the BCP and founded the Union of Black Journalists. Banned in 1973, he served a short term of imprisonment for breaking his banning order. Later that year he left for exile for 20 years, 17 of them in France where he survived as a taxi driver. Later he worked as a freelance journalist for Radio France International and *Le Monde Diplomatique*. He currently works as a writer.

Mosibudi Mangena was born in Tzaneen in 1947. He became a member of SASO in 1970 at the University of Zululand, where he was studying towards a BSc degree. He was elected National Organiser of the Black People's Convention in 1972. In 1973 he was sentenced to five years' imprisonment on Robben Island under the Terrorism Act. On release in 1978 he was banished to Mahwelereng township near Mokopane. He went into exile in 1981 and joined the Black Consciousness Movement of Azania (BCMA) in Botswana. He was later elected chairperson of the BCMA and moved to Zimbabwe. On his return to South Africa in 1994 he was elected president of the Azanian People's Organisation, a position he still holds. He was elected to Parliament in 1999 and appointed Deputy Minister of Education in 2001. After the 2004 election he was appointed Minister of Science and Technology. Mosibudi has written four books: *On Your Own, The Quest For True Humanity, A Twin World,* and *My Grandmother Is Permanent.*

Thabo Mbeki was born in 1942 in Mbewuleni, a tiny village in the Idutywa district of the Eastern Cape. He attended high school at Lovedale but was expelled as a result of student strikes in 1959. He continued his studies at home and wrote his matriculation at St John's High School in Umtata that same year. In 1962 he went into exile, returning to South Africa in 1990 after the release of Nelson Mandela.

Mbeki spent the early years of his exile in the United Kingdom, earning a Master of Economics degree from the University of Sussex and then working in the ANC's London office. He became the ANC's Director of Information in 1978. He received military training in the then Soviet Union and lived at different times in Botswana, Swaziland and Nigeria, but his primary base was in Lusaka, Zambia, the site of the ANC headquarters. He became a deputy president of South Africa in May 1994 and sole deputy president in June 1996. He succeeded Nelson Mandela as ANC president in December 1997 and as President of the Republic in 1999. He was re-elected in April 2004.

Veli Mbele was born in 1976 in the township of Galeshewe, near Kimberley. After attending Zingisa Primary School and Tshireleco High in Galeshewe he started his tertiary studies at the former Free State Technikon (now the Central University of Technology) and went on to the Peninsula Technikon (now the Cape University of Technology). He is currently Deputy Director for Parliamentary Affairs in the office of the Minister of Science and Technology.

Achille Mbembe was born in Cameroon. He obtained his PhD in history at the University of Paris (Pantheon-Sorbonne) and a DEA in politics at the Institut d'Etudes Politiques, Paris. From 1988 to 1991 he was an Assistant Professor in history at Columbia University, New York. He spent a year as a Senior Fellow at The Brookings Institute, Washington, DC before joining the University of Pennsylvania, Philadelphia, as an Associate Professor in history from 1993 to 1996. From 1996 to 2000 he was Director of the Council for the Development of Social Science Research in Africa (CODESRIA). He has taught at various universities in the United States and in France, including the University of California at Berkeley, the University of California at Irvine, Yale University, the University of Chicago and the Ecole des Hautes Etudes en Sciences Sociales (Paris). He joined the University of the Witwatersrand as a Senior Researcher at the Wits Institute for Social and Economic Research in 2001 and was appointed a Research Professor in history and politics in 2003. He is the author of more than 50 articles in international scientific journals and has published four books, the latest of which, *On the Postcolony*, has appeared in French, English and Italian and won the Bill Venter/Altron Award for 2006.

Lizeka Mda was born in Mthatha in 1964, but spent most of her childhood years in the land of amaGcaleka, in the Gatyana district. She came to Johannesburg in 1985 to work on *Upbeat* magazine, an educational magazine for teenagers. She has a BA Honours degree in Journalism and Sociology from Rhodes University and an Associateship in Children's Literature from the Institute of Education, London University. She has worked as a journalist since 1985, mostly in magazines and newspapers and has also compiled radio programmes for the British and Canadian Broadcasting Corporations, did a monthly column on SABC radio's current-affairs program, 'PM Live', between 1997 and 2003, and was occasional host of Radio 702's 'Talk at 9' evening show. She has had works of fiction and non-fiction published and has presented papers at international conferences, with a special focus on African media. She is a Nieman Fellow and spent an academic year at Harvard University in 2003/2004, concentrating on globalisation.

Pandelani Nefolovhodwe MP and Deputy President of Azapo, was born in 1947 in Folovhodwe in Limpopo. He attended school in Venda and in 1969 enrolled at the University of the North (Turfloop) for a BSc degree. In 1971 he became a member of the SRC and in 1972 was expelled from Turfloop for protesting against the expulsion of Onkgopotse Tiro. In 1974 he re-enrolled at Turfloop and was elected SRC President. In the same year he was elected SASO National President and was later arrested for organising Viva Frelimo rallies. Convicted on terrorism charges at the SASO/BPC trial, he served six years on Robben Island. In 1983, he joined the Black Allied Mining and Construction Workers Union (BAMCWU) as regional organiser for Limpopo and was elected Secretary General in 1984. He founded the National Council of Trade Unions in 1986 and was its first Assistant Secretary General. In 1990 he became Secretary General of the newly unbanned Azapo and, in 1990, National President.

Mandla Seleoane, born in 1951, grew up in Middelburg (Transvaal, as it was). He studied at the University of South Africa, the Rand Afrikaans University and the University of Stellenbosch. He has worked as a researcher with the

Surplus People's Project, documenting Southern Africa Labour and Development Research at the University of Cape Town, as Education Officer for Labour at the Wilgespruit Fellowship Centre and as a researcher at the Human Sciences Research Council. He is currently employed by the Tshwane University of Technology. He writes a weekly column entitled 'No Holy Cows' for the *Herald* in Port Elizabeth. Seleoane received the HSRC REXCEL award for 'outstanding work in research in the human sciences' in 1996, the Caldwell Unconventional Hero Award for 'principled and courageous defence of freedom of speech' in 1997, a Certificate of Appreciation for 'outstanding contribution towards making Technikon North West a success' in 2003. He has published two books and co-edited another with Jane Duncan, and has had articles published in academic journals.

Mathatha Tsedu, currently Editor in Chief of *City Press*, was born in Makhado town in Limpopo in 1952. He matriculated from Mphaphuli High and recently completed a BA Hons at Wits University. He was previously Editor of the *Sunday Times*, Deputy Head of News at the South African Broadcasting Corporation, Deputy Editor of *The Star* and the *Sunday Independent*, Political Editor of the *Sowetan* and was chairperson of the South African Editors' Forum for three consecutive years.